PERFECT
PASTA&RICE

WINDWARD

Published by Windward, an imprint owned by
W.H. Smith & Son Limited
Registered No. 237811 England
Trading as WHS Distributors,
St John's House, East Street, Leicester LE1.6NE

© Marshall Cavendish Limited 1985

ISBN 0-7112-0409 8

Printed and bound in Hong Kong by
Dai Nippon Printing Company

CONTENTS

ALL ABOUT PASTA

Not only is pasta inexpensive, it is also quick and simple to cook and provides a tasty way of stretching meat and vegetables to make complete nutritious meals. The range of pasta now available, both fresh and dried, means more menu variety for family meals.

Pasta is made from a hard variety of wheat called durum wheat which absorbs less water than other wheats when cooked. Pasta is available dried and fresh.

DRIED PASTA

Moisture has been removed from pasta to make dried pasta. If it has been made with the addition of egg yolk it will be labelled *all'uovo* on packets.

Allow 50 g/2 oz per person as a first course and 100-175 g/ 4-6 oz per person for a main course, depending on the dish being made.

Buying guide: dried pasta is available in supermarkets; Italian delicatessens stock a wider range of different dried shapes. Check the label carefully before buying. The best dried pasta comes from southern Italy where it is widely made and eaten.

Storage: store in a cool, dry place. Dried pasta keeps almost indefinitely, but is best used within 1 year.

Cooking: Most pasta should be cooked in boiling salted water, but cooking times will vary according to the type of pasta and shape. Whichever type, pasta should be cooked until tender but firm to the bite, what the Italians call *al dente* (literally, 'to the tooth'). Test by biting a piece.

For every 225 g/8 oz dried pasta use about 2.25 L/4 pints cold water and 1 tablespoon salt. Bring the water to the boil, swirl about 2 teaspoons oil over the top, then add the pasta and simmer until cooked (see opposite for individual cooking times). Drain in a colander and turn at once into a large warmed bowl. Toss the pasta in a knob of butter or oil and serve at once with a sauce or alternatively, toss pasta in prepared sauce.

FRESH PASTA

Usually made with the addition of egg yolks, this is the favourite pasta eaten in northern Italy.

Allow 100 g/4 oz per person for a first course and 175-225 g/6-8 oz per person for a main course.

Buying guide: it is sold loose by the kg/lb in delicatessens and in packets in most large supermarkets.

Storage: keep wrapped in the refrigerator and use within 2 days. To freeze, divide into convenient-sized portions, pack in a rigid container, seal, label and freeze for up to 3 months. Defrost completely before cooking.

Cooking: fresh pasta is cooked in the same way as dried pasta except it requires much less cooking time. If stuck together, carefully pull strands of pasta apart before adding to boiling water. Cook for 3-4 minutes.

PASTA VARIETIES

Pasta may be flavoured and coloured. All are available both fresh and dried. Green pasta has been made with spinach added to the dough; it is known as *pasta verde* or *pasta al spinaci*. Use for serving with tomato and/or cheese sauces, but avoid serving it with delicate sauces as the strong flavour of the spinach may be overpowering.

An unusual pasta is *pasta pomodoro*, which has been coloured with tomato purée. Avoid serving this pasta with red tomato sauces as it looks unappetizing.

Wholewheat pasta is made with wholewheat flour and has more fibre than ordinary pasta. It has a nutty flavour. Use as for green pasta. The widest selection is in health food stores but supermarkets stock it as well.

Pasta shapes are labelled in Italian or English. Also manufacturers use Italian names for their own shapes.

Cannelloni: (1) these large cylinders of fried pasta are intended for stuffing with meat, fish or cheese mixtures. They are then baked with a sauce. Cook as for lasagne (see below) before stuffing, or look for pre-cooked types.

Lasagne: (2) sheets of lasagne are used for layering with meat and cheese to make the classic Italian *lasagne al forno*. They can also be rolled up to make cannelloni (see above).

Lasagne is sold in wide flat sheets and in squares, which are easier to fit into a baking dish. Corrugated narrow sheets are sold and will not stick together when cooked.

Cook dried lasagne for 10-12 minutes until just tender, then drop in a bowl of cold water to prevent sticking.

Fresh lasagne should be cooked for about 1 minute before baking.

Pre-cooked lasagne is an excellent time-saver because, as its name implies, it does not need to be boiled first.

Macaroni: Italian macaroni are long thin tubes of pasta, **(3)** but most macaroni sold here is short-cut **(4)** for easy cooking; it is only available dried, either plain or wholewheat. Most often used to make macaroni cheese, it can be combined with other sauces such as tomato or added when cooked to soups and casseroles. Cook short-cut macaroni for 20 minutes; quick-cooking thin-cut macaroni cooks in 6 minutes and is best reserved for making sweet puddings.

Ravioli: (5) these squares of pasta are filled with either a minced meat mixture or Ricotta cheese which is sometimes mixed with spinach. They are available fresh from delicatessens and large supermarkets. Canned ravioli is sold in supermarkets; dried ravioli is also sold. Cook fresh ravioli for 5-7 minutes, or

according to packet instructions, and serve either with a tomato sauce or toss in butter and grated cheese.

Soup pasta: (6) miniature shapes ranging from star to teardrop shapes. Cook in stock and serve as a simple soup, called *pasta in brodo* in Italy. Larger shapes should be cooked for 5 minutes before adding to soup to prevent it from turning cloudy.

Spaghetti: (7) spaghetti is available in various lengths and widths but is always round. Cook spaghetti according to packet instructions. Long thin spaghetti imported from Italy **(8)** and sold in blue wrappers takes about 10 minutes to cook. Fresh spaghetti is available, as is also the slightly wider *tagliarini* or *tagliolini* **(9)** which may be used in the same way. Cook 2-3 minutes.

Vermicelli are very narrow spaghetti, and are sold dried in nests. Cook 5 minutes and serve with a sauce or break into pieces and add to soups.

Spaghetti should be lowered vertically into boiling water and as it softens the rest pushed down into the pan. Serve with tomato sauces, especially bolognese.

Tagliatelle: (10) also known as ribbon noodles because of their flat shape, this pasta also comes in varying widths. *Fettucine* **(11)**, some say, is

narrower. These are the best noodles to serve with rich sauces and, in fact, are good served simply tossed in butter with grated cheese and cream added. Serve in place of potatoes, especially with stews and casseroles.

Packets of mixed plain and green tagliatelle are sold. In Italy this is called *paglia e fieno*, or straw and hay.

Tortelloni: (12), cappelletti (13): these stuffed pastas along with smaller *tortellini* are among the increasing variety of tasty alternatives to ravioli now available. Cook and serve as for ravioli (left), or according to packet instructions. Dried tortellini is also sold.

Other pasta shapes: bows **(14)**, wheels **(15)**, spirals **(16)**, shells **(17)** or any of the vast number of interesting shapes make excellent store-cupboard items. Cook as instructed on packet; serve with meaty sauces. Alternatively, use to make pasta salads.

ALL ABOUT RICE

Countries around the world have long appreciated the nutritional and economical value of rice. In this country we have a variety of rices to choose from – each with their own special uses. Follow our guidelines for choosing the right rice; opposite we tell you how to cook it – perfectly.

Rice contributes protein, some of the B vitamins and a variety of minerals such as potassium, calcium and magnesium to the diet. Brown rice and parboiled rice contain more of the B vitamins than other rices.

BUYING GUIDE AND STORAGE

Rice available in supermarkets comes mainly from America and the remainder from India and Italy. The country of origin will be marked on the pack. Always make sure, if you can see them, that the grains of rice are unbroken and that there is no sediment in the pack.

Stored in a cool, dark place, rice will keep for 1 year.

TYPES

Follow the guidelines set out below for choosing rice:

Brown rice: rice is processed to remove the outer inedible husk. This first stage of processing yields brown rice which may have a long **(1)** or short **(2)** grain. It has a nutty flavour and is more filling than white rice. Use in place of white rice for most dishes but avoid those where its strong flavour may be overpowering such as in curries and paellas. Brown rice takes about twice as long to cook as white rice.

Short-grain rice or pudding rice (3): this is rice which is traditionally used to make sweet rice puddings as well as creamy moulds. The grains are fat and oval and become sticky when cooked.

Medium-grain rice or risotto rice (4): these are more round than long, and are characterized by being able to absorb a lot of liquid without becoming soft or sticky. They are ideal for making risottos, which require long cooking.

The easy-cook rice from Italy sold in supermarkets is suitable for risottos but for the best risotto rice look for *Arborio* **(5)** and *Avorio* **(6)** rice sold in Italian delicatessens.

Long-grain rice: this is the rice used for savoury dishes. It has clear translucent grains about four times longer than they are wide. When cooked, the rice is light and fluffy and the grains remain completely separate.

Most long-grain rice comes from America. *Patna* long-grain **(7)** rice is from India, but rice labelled 'patna-style' is not necessarily Indian. *Basmati* rice **(8)** is another Indian rice renowned for its distinctive full flavour. It is the ideal – and authentic – rice for curries and pilaus. Unlike other rice, basmati rice must be rinsed before it is cooked to remove excess starch and it takes less time to cook than other rices.

Parboiled, easy-cook, pre-fluffed or separate grain rice (9): is usually long-grain rice which has been steam treated under pressure before the husk has been removed. The process helps to retain some of the vitamins and minerals which would normally be removed with the husk and germ. Processing also helps the grains to remain separate when cooked. The rice is yellowish in colour, but turns white on cooking. Cook according to packet instructions and use as for ordinary long-grain rice.

Pre-cooked or canned rice (10): this rice has been fully cooked and coated in oil to keep the grains separate. It is then packed into cans. It only needs to be heated through, which takes just 3 minutes. Canned rice is convenient for camping trips. It is sold in supermarkets.

Flaked rice (11): here the grains have been flaked. They cook quickly and are convenient for puddings.

Ground rice (12) and rice flour (13): for ground rice, grains are ground to a coarse powder; rice flour is finely ground grains. Ground rice is used in puddings, similar to semolina, and in biscuits, especially shortbread. It is also a good thickener of soups and sauces. Rice flour may be added to cakes and biscuits.

Wild rice (14): this is not really rice but the seeds of an aquatic plant that grows in North America. Though very expensive it has an unusual nutty flavour that is wonderful in poultry stuffings. Cook according to packet instructions. Available in high-class food shops. Mixed wild rice and long-grain rice **(15)** is sold in supermarkets and is less expensive.

COOKING

The one golden rule when cooking rice is not to stir it during cooking or it will become starchy. Rice should be cooked until firm but not too soft. Test by biting a grain between the teeth – it should offer some resistance. Allow 50 g/2 oz raw rice per person.

Total absorption method: this is by far the best way to cook rice as it is the most reliable. Simply weigh out the amount of rice you require, put into a measuring jug, then use double the volume of liquid for cooking.

Transfer rice and water to a saucepan and add salt – ½ teaspoon per 50 g/2 oz. Bring to the boil, stir once, cover pan tightly and then simmer over low heat for 15 minutes without removing the lid (30-40 minutes for brown rice). After this time

all the liquid should have been absorbed; the rice should be quite separate and the grains easily fluffed up with a fork.

Excess water method: this is a good method to use if you have a large bag of rice that has tended to cook to a sticky mass – it will most likely be a poor quality rice.

Add the rice to a pan of boiling salted water. Stir once, cover and simmer for 5-7 minutes. Towards the end of cooking time, test the rice. It should be still quite firm to the bite, drain quickly, rinse under cold water to stop further cooking, then return to the rinsed-out pan and leave the rice to completely dry out over very low heat for about 10 minutes. Alternatively, put the rice in a greased baking dish and allow the rice to dry in a 180C/350F/Gas 4 oven for

approximately 10 minutes.

Oven method: this method is useful if you are cooking other food in the oven at the same time. Measure the rice and water in the same way as for the total absorption method. Place the rice and salt in a casserole dish with a close-fitting lid. Bring the water to the boil and pour it over the rice. Cover and cook in a 180C/350F/Gas 4 oven for about 40 minutes until the grains are tender and fluffy and all the water has been absorbed. Fluff up the rice with a fork and serve.

Steamed rice: use this method for rice served with Chinese-style meals: cook rice using excess water method above for less than 10 minutes until rice is still firm. Drain thoroughly and wrap the rice in a double thickness of muslin or a very clean tea-towel. Place the bundle in

a steamer basket over boiling water, cover tightly then steam for 20-25 minutes until rice is tender. Alternatively, a colander or sieve may be used just as effectively.

Special bamboo baskets for steaming rice are sold in Chinese shops and some department stores. Electric steamers are also sold. Follow manufacturer's instructions.

TRADITIONAL RICE DISHES

Chinese-style fried rice: fully cooked cold long-grain rice is stir-fried in oil over high heat. Season with soy sauce, finely chopped spring onions and ginger. Shellfish, chicken or egg strips may be added.

Paella: traditional Spanish paellas are slowly cooked in a special shallow pan called a *paellera* but a wide frying-pan can be used. Risotto rice is first lightly fried in oil, before being cooked in stock. Essential ingredients include shellfish, tomatoes and garlic. The paella is also flavoured and coloured with saffron.

Risotto: traditionally eaten as a first course in Italy, risottos can be made into substantial dishes with the addition of meat and vegetables which are cooked along with the rice. Stock is added to the rice gradually: each time liquid must be absorbed by the rice before the next addition of liquid, which is why it is essential to use risotto rice (see previous page).

Pilaffs or pilaus: long-grain rice is first fried in a fat, then stock is added and seasonings. For Indian pilau rice, use basmati rice and season well with curry spices. With Middle Eastern pilaffs, rice is first fried in olive oil. The pilaffs are traditionally flavoured with pistachio nuts or pine nuts and raisins.

SOUPS AND STARTERS

Minestrone

Italian Minestrone is one of the world's great soups. Made from different mixed vegetables with cooked pulses and either small pasta shapes or rice added, it is a thick soup that is nourishing and filling.

A warming bowlful of minestrone sprinkled with grated Parmesan cheese is perfect for a cold wintry day, but in fact it was originally a summer soup. Equally good served hot or cold (but not chilled), it always seems to taste even better the day after it is made. For the very best flavour, do not serve the soup piping hot, but allow it to cool slightly first so that the flavour has time to develop and 'mature'.

The secret of good minestrone is to use really fresh vegetables which are cooked in olive oil to start with (the Italians call this stage *soffrito*), then simmered very gently for a long time, so that all their goodness and flavour comes through. Frozen vegetables should not be used for making minestrone: they give unsatisfactory results.

SERVES 8

2 tablespoons olive oil (see Did you know)
50 g/2 oz back bacon, rinds removed and finely chopped
2 tablespoons chopped parsley
1 clove garlic, finely chopped
¼ cabbage (weighing 150 g/5 oz), roughly shredded (see Preparation)
100 g/4 oz spinach, cut into small, thin strips (see Preparation)
1 large potato, diced
1 large courgette, sliced
1 carrot, diced
1 onion, chopped
1 celery stalk, sliced

400 g/14 oz can tomatoes, chopped, with their juice
2 L/3½ pints vegetable or chicken stock
salt and freshly ground black pepper
100 g/4 oz small pasta shells or short-cut macaroni (see Buying guide)
400 g/14 oz can white cannellini beans, drained and rinsed
75 g/3 oz Parmesan cheese, finely grated, to serve

1 Heat the olive oil in a large saucepan, add the bacon and cook gently for 2-3 minutes, stirring all the time.
2 Add the parsley and garlic and cook for a further 2-3 minutes, stirring all the time.
3 Add all the vegetables except the tomatoes and the canned beans and cook for a further 4-5 minutes,

continuing to stir all the time, so that the vegetables do not catch.
4 Add the tomatoes with their juice and the stock and bring to the boil. Lower the heat and add salt and pepper to taste. Cover and simmer very gently for about 1½ hours, stirring occasionally. ✳
5 Bring the soup back to the boil, add the pasta, and bring back to the boil again. Simmer for about 15 minutes or until the pasta is almost cooked.
6 Add the beans and continue to cook for a few minutes until the pasta is tender. Taste and adjust seasoning.
7 Allow the soup to stand for 10-15 minutes for the flavour to develop, then ladle into warmed soup bowls. Serve with grated Parmesan cheese handed separately in a small bowl.

Frankfurter and vegetable soup

SERVES 6

100 g/4 oz frankfurters, cut into 5
   mm/¼ inch slices
2 tablespoons vegetable oil
175 g/6 oz carrots, cut into 1 cm/½
   inch dice
1 celery stalk, thinly sliced
250 g/9 oz turnips, cut into 1 cm/½
   inch dice
1 onion, chopped
1 clove garlic, crushed (optional)
700 ml/1¼ pints beef stock
400 g/14 oz can chopped tomatoes
salt and freshly ground black pepper
50 g/2 oz green cabbage leaves,
   shredded
25 g/1 oz pasta (see Buying guide)
50 g/2 oz Cheddar cheese, grated

1 Heat the oil in a heavy-based
saucepan, add the carrots, celery,
turnips, onion and garlic, if using,
and cook over moderate heat for 7
minutes, stirring.

2 Remove from the heat and stir in
the stock and tomatoes. Season to
taste with salt and pepper.
3 Return the pan to the heat and
bring to the boil. Lower the heat,
cover the pan and simmer for 20
minutes.
4 Add the cabbage and pasta, then
cover again and simmer for a further

10 minutes until the pasta is soft.
5 Stir in the frankfurters, taste and
adjust seasoning, and cook for a
further 3 minutes.
6 Ladle into warmed individual
bowls or a soup tureen and serve at
once. Hand the grated cheese in a
separate bowl for sprinkling on top
of the soup.

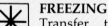

Chinese leafy soup

SERVES 4

850 ml/1½ pints chicken stock
1 bunch spring onions, finely shredded diagonally including the green tops
1 teaspoon finely grated fresh root ginger (see Buying guide)
2 teaspoons lemon juice
2 teaspoons soy sauce
salt and freshly ground black pepper
50 g/2 oz Chinese fine egg noodles
2-3 lettuce leaves, finely shredded and chopped
½ bunch watercress, divided into small sprigs and chopped

1 Heat the stock until on the point of boiling, then add just over half of the spring onions together with the grated ginger, lemon juice and soy sauce. Half cover with a lid and simmer gently for 5 minutes.

2 Meanwhile, bring a pan of salted water to the boil and cook the egg noodles for 6 minutes until tender.

3 Add the lettuce and watercress to the chicken stock and simmer for a further 5 minutes. Adjust seasoning, if necessary, transfer to a warmed serving bowl and garnish with the remaining spring onions.

4 Drain the noodles thoroughly, then divide equally between 4 warmed individual soup bowls. Spoon the soup into the bowls of noodles and serve at once.

Cook's Notes

 TIME
This soup takes only 30 minutes to make.

 SERVING IDEAS
Serve as a starter for a Chinese-type meal or as a low-calorie snack with crispbreads or Melba toast followed by fresh fruit.

 VARIATIONS
Add a little chopped, cooked chicken or a few chopped, peeled prawns a few minutes just before the end of cooking time.

 ECONOMY
This is an ideal soup for leftovers: use lettuce leaves and sprigs of watercress from a salad and stock made from a chicken carcass.

 BUYING GUIDE
Fresh or 'green' ginger is the root of the ginger plant; it is now widely available in good greengrocers and supermarkets, as well as the more specialized Chinese food stores. Peel before grating.

● 70 calories/275 kj per portion

Carrot soup with egg and rice

SERVES 4

750 g/1½ lb new carrots, thinly
   sliced
25 g/1 oz margarine or butter
600 ml/1 pint chicken stock
1 teaspoon sugar
salt and freshly ground black pepper
150 ml/¼ pint milk
75 g/3 oz cooked rice (see Cook's
   tips)
4 eggs at room temperature (see
   Cook's tips)
2 spring onions, finely chopped
150 ml/¼ pint single cream

1 Melt the margarine in a saucepan,
add the carrots and fry gently for
2-3 minutes to soften slightly.
2 Add the chicken stock and sugar
and season to taste with salt and
pepper. Bring to the boil, then
lower the heat and simmer, uncovered, for 30 minutes or until the
carrots are very tender.
3 Remove the pan from the heat
and allow mixture to cool slightly,
then pour it into the goblet of a
blender and work for a few seconds
until smooth. Return the purée to
the rinsed-out pan and stir in the
milk and the cooked rice. Taste and
adjust the seasoning, if necessary.
4 Heat the soup gently until hot but
not boiling, then break in the eggs
and poach them for about 8 minutes
or until they are firm enough to be
lifted out with a slotted spoon.
5 Spoon an egg into each of 4
warmed soup bowls and pour over
the soup. Sprinkle over the spring
onions, swirl in the cream and serve
the soup at once.

Cook's Notes

TIME
Preparation takes 15
minutes, cooking takes
about 50 minutes.

SERVING IDEAS
This is a fairly substan-
tial soup, so serve with
a light accompaniment such as
Melba toast or a selection of
crispbreads.

COOK'S TIPS
If cooking raw rice for
this dish, you will need
25 g/1 oz to provide 75 g/3 oz of
cooked rice.

Remove the eggs from the
refrigerator 1 hour before using:
cold eggs will require a longer
time to set.

● 155 calories/650 kj per portion

Tomato rice soup

SERVES 4

500 g/1 lb fresh tomatoes, chopped
400 g/14 oz can tomatoes
1 tablespoon tomato purée
150 ml/¼ pint water
salt and freshly ground black pepper
50 g/2 oz long-grain rice
2 tablespoons medium sherry
   (optional, see Variation)
1 tablespoon finely chopped
   parsley, to garnish

1 Put all the ingredients except the rice, sherry, if using, and parsley into a large saucepan. Bring to the boil, stirring, then lower the heat, cover and simmer for 30 minutes.

2 Pass the contents of the saucepan through a sieve, or leave to cool slightly, then purée in a blender and sieve (see Cook's tip).

3 Pour the sieved tomato purée back into the rinsed-out pan and bring back to the boil. Stir in the rice, lower the heat, cover and simmer for about 15 minutes or until the rice is tender.

4 Stir in the sherry, if using, taste and adjust seasoning, then pour into warmed individual soup bowls. Sprinkle with parsley and serve at once.

Cook's Notes

TIME
Preparation and cooking take about 1 hour.

VARIATION
Use 2 tablespoons single cream instead of the sherry, and swirl a little into each bowl just before sprinkling with parsley.

SERVING IDEAS
Serve with hot wholemeal rolls.

COOK'S TIP
It is essential to sieve the tomato mixture, to remove the pips and skins.

●80 calories/325 kj per portion

Spaghetti with anchovy sauce

SERVES 8
500 g/1 lb spaghetti
salt
1 teaspoon vegetable oil
25 g/1 oz butter

ANCHOVY SAUCE
2 tablespoons vegetable oil
1 clove garlic, crushed (optional)
1 large onion, finely chopped
50 g/2 oz can anchovy fillets in oil,
  mashed to a paste
2 teaspoons plain flour
400 g/14 oz can chopped tomatoes
2 teaspoons tomato purée
2 teaspoons dried basil
freshly ground black pepper

1 Bring a large pan of salted water to the boil, swirl in the oil and add the spaghetti. Bring back to the boil then lower the heat and simmer for 10-12 minutes or until the spaghetti is quite tender yet firm to the bite.

2 Meanwhile, make anchovy sauce: heat the oil in a heavy-based sauce-pan, add the garlic, if using, and onion and fry very gently for 7 minutes until golden.
3 Stir the anchovy paste and flour into the onion and cook, stirring, for a further 2 minutes. Gradually blend in the chopped tomatoes and their juices, the tomato purée and basil. Add pepper to taste and

simmer gently for 8-10 minutes, stirring occasionally.
4 Drain the pasta thoroughly, then return to the rinsed-out pan. Add the butter and season well with pepper. Toss over gentle heat until spaghetti is coated in butter.
5 Transfer the spaghetti to warmed serving plates and top with the anchovy sauce. Serve at once. For a finishing touch, see Serving ideas.

Spaghetti supreme

SERVES 6
250 g/9 oz wholewheat spaghetti
salt
1 teaspoon vegetable oil
50 g/2 oz butter
200 g/7 oz blue Stilton cheese, cut
    into small cubes
25 g/1 oz walnut pieces, roughly
    chopped
150 ml/¼ pint single cream
freshly ground black pepper
65 g/2½ oz watercress, trimmed of
    thick stalks, finely chopped

1 Bring a large saucepan of salted water to the boil. Swirl in the oil, then add the spaghetti. Bring back to the boil and simmer for about 20 minutes, until the spaghetti is tender but still firm to the bite.

2 Meanwhile, melt the butter in a small saucepan. Add the Stilton and cook over very low heat, mashing with a wooden spoon, until the cheese has melted. Remove the pan from the heat and then stir in the chopped walnuts. Gradually add the cream, stirring vigorously. Season with a little salt and plenty of pepper. Set aside until just before the spaghetti is ready to serve.

3 Return the sauce to low heat, add the watercress and warm through. ⚠

4 Drain the spaghetti and rinse with boiling water. Drain again and transfer to a warmed serving dish. Pour over the sauce and then toss gently until the spaghetti is evenly coated with sauce. Serve the dish at once.

Cook's Notes

 TIME
Preparation takes about 30 minutes.

⚠ **WATCHPOINT**
Warm the cheese sauce through gently – it will separate if it becomes too hot. If this does happen, remove pan from heat and beat the sauce with a wooden spoon until it is thick and creamy.

 VARIATION
Try other shapes of wholewheat pasta, such as macaroni or shells or tagliatelle.

SERVING IDEAS
This is quite a rich and filling starter so follow it with a light main course.

●625 calories/2600 kj per portion

Roman salad

SERVES 6
250 g/9 oz green tagliatelle (see Variation)
salt
1 teaspoon vegetable oil
200 g/7 oz can tuna in oil, drained, flaked and oil reserved
4 hard-boiled eggs, chopped
2 tomatoes, skinned and chopped
45 g/1¾ oz can anchovy fillets, drained, soaked in milk for 20 minutes, drained and chopped
4 celery stalks, chopped

HERB DRESSING
3 tablespoons vegetable oil
1 tablespoon white wine vinegar
1 teaspoon lemon juice
1 clove garlic, crushed (optional)
pinch of sugar
1 teaspoon finely chopped fresh basil
1 tablespoon finely chopped parsley
freshly ground black pepper

1 Bring a large pan of salted water to the boil, swirl in the oil and add the tagliatelle. Bring back to the boil and cook for 7-10 minutes (or according to packet instructions), until tender yet firm to the bite.
2 Meanwhile, make herb dressing: put the reserved oil from the can of tuna into a screw-top jar with the rest of the dressing ingredients, adding salt and pepper to taste. Replace the lid firmly and shake the dressing thoroughly until completely blended.
3 Drain the pasta, rinse under cold running water and drain again thoroughly.
4 Put the cooked pasta in a salad bowl. Add the tuna, chopped hard-boiled eggs, tomatoes, anchovies and celery. Pour over the herb dressing and toss the ingredients lightly together: Serve at once (see Serving ideas).

16

Tagliatelle in parsley sauce

SERVES 6

350 g/12 oz fresh tagliatelle (see Buying guide)
1 tablespoon vegetable oil
grated Parmesan cheese, to serve

SAUCE
100 g/4 oz fresh parsley sprigs
2 large cloves garlic, chopped
25 g/1 oz pine kernels (see Buying guide)
150 ml/¼ pint olive oil (see Economy)
salt
50 g/2 oz Parmesan cheese, grated
freshly ground black pepper

1 First make the sauce: put the parsley, garlic, pine kernels and oil into a blender (see Cook's tips). Add pinch of salt and purée for 1 minute. Add all of the grated Parmesan cheese and purée for 1 minute more,

then season with pepper to taste.
2 Bring a large pan of salted water to the boil. Add the oil and tagliatelle and stir once. Bring back to the boil and cook for 2-3 minutes until *al dente* (tender, yet firm to the bite).
3 Drain the tagliatelle well, then turn into a warmed serving dish. Stir the sauce and add to the dish. Quickly toss the tagliatelle with 2 forks to mix it with the sauce. Serve at once while still hot, with a bowl filled with grated Parmesan cheese handed separately.

Cook's Notes

TIME
Preparation and cooking take about 30 minutes.

ECONOMY
Use half olive and half vegetable oil.

COOK'S TIPS
If you do not have a blender, pound the garlic, nuts and salt to a paste in a mortar, then slowly work in the parsley, cheese and oil.

Store the sauce in a covered container in the refrigerator for a few days. Bring to room temperature before using.

BUYING GUIDE
Remember you can buy fresh tagliatelle (or egg noodles) from Italian delicatessens and some supermarkets. If fresh tagliatelle is unavailable you can use the dried type and cook according to packet instructions.

Pine kernels, sold in health food stores, are small tapering nuts with a soft, oily texture and resinous flavour. Alternatively, you can buy unsalted cashew nuts if you prefer a milder taste.

● 735 calories/3075 kj per portion

Mushroom and ham medley

SERVES 6

250 g/9 oz button mushrooms, chopped (see Buying guide)
salt
1 teaspoon vegetable oil
25 g/1 oz pasta shells or bows
300 ml/½ pint chicken stock
25 g/1 oz margarine or butter
25 g/1 oz plain flour
300 ml/½ pint milk
200 g/7 oz can sweetcorn, drained
100 g/4 oz cooked ham, diced
freshly ground black pepper
2 tablespoons chopped fresh parsley, to garnish

1 Bring a large pan of salted water to the boil, swirl in the oil, then add the pasta. Bring back to the boil and cook for 7-10 minutes until tender but firm to the bite.

2 Meanwhile, in a separate large saucepan, heat the stock with the margarine until boiling. Add the mushrooms, lower the heat and simmer for up to 5 minutes until the mushrooms have softened.

3 Put the flour in a bowl, then gradually whisk in the milk with a balloon whisk. Stir the milk and flour mixture into the mushrooms in the saucepan, bring to the boil, then lower the heat and simmer for a few minutes, stirring.

4 Drain the pasta and stir into the mushroom mixture with the sweetcorn and ham. Season to taste with salt and pepper and heat through very gently, stirring occasionally.

5 Pour into warmed individual soup bowls and sprinkle with parsley. Serve at once.

Savoury pasta

SERVES 6-8
225 g/8 oz pasta shapes
salt
few drops of vegetable oil
100 g/4 oz streaky bacon, derinded
   and finely chopped
1 large onion, thinly sliced
3 tablespoons plain flour
1 teaspoon mustard powder
425 ml/¾ pint warm milk
4 sage leaves, chopped, or
   1 teaspoon dried sage
3 tablespoons chopped parsley
freshly ground black pepper
3 egg yolks
200 g/7 oz Cheddar cheese, grated
2 tablespoons wheatgerm (see
   Buying guide)

1 Heat the oven to 200C/400F/Gas 6.
2 Bring a large saucepan of salted water to the boil, add the oil, then add the pasta and stir well. Bring back to the boil, lower the heat and cook for about 10 minutes until the pasta is *al dente* (tender, yet firm to the bite).
3 Meanwhile, put the bacon in a large saucepan, place over low heat and cook until the fat begins to run. Add the onion, raise the heat and cook until the onion is softened.
4 Sprinkle in the flour and mustard powder, then stir over low heat for 2 minutes. Remove from the heat and gradually stir in the milk. Return to the heat and simmer, stirring, until thick and smooth. Add the herbs and salt and pepper to taste.
5 Remove the pan from the heat and beat in the egg yolks one at a time.

Drain the pasta and stir into the sauce with two-thirds of the cheese.
6 Pile the mixture into a large ovenproof dish and smooth the top. Cover with the remaining cheese and sprinkle the wheatgerm over the top.
7 Bake in the oven for 25 minutes, then place under a heated grill for a few minutes to brown. Serve at once.

Cook's Notes

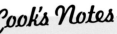

 TIME
This dish can be prepared and cooked in just under 1 hour.

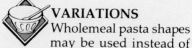 **VARIATIONS**
Wholemeal pasta shapes may be used instead of plain pasta.
The bacon may be omitted and 25 g/1 oz margarine used for frying the onion instead.

BUYING GUIDE
It is worth buying wheatgerm specially for this dish, as it not only gives a good texture to the topping but is also an excellent source of proteins, fats and vitamins D and E. Wheatgerm is available from health food shops, but if you cannot obtain it, use the same quantity of wholemeal breadcrumbs instead.

 COOK'S TIP
If you are careful to mix the pasta and sauce together quickly while they are both still hot, then there is no need to bake this dish in the oven to heat through. It will be hot enough if just put under the grill until the top is golden brown.

●455 calories/1900 kj per portion

Salami shell salad

SERVES 6-8
250 g/9 oz pasta wheels or shells
salt
1 teaspoon vegetable oil
175 g/6 oz salami, cut into strips
    4 cm/1½ inches long and
    1 cm/½ inch wide
8 spring onions, each cut into
    4 lengths
400 g/14 oz can artichoke hearts,
    drained, rinsed and halved
    (see Variations)
50 g/2 oz black olives
2 tomatoes, each cut into 8 wedges
lettuce leaves, to serve

DRESSING
3 tablespoons vegetable oil
1 tablespoon white wine vinegar
½ teaspoon sugar
½ teaspoon mustard powder
freshly ground black pepper

1 Bring a large pan of salted water to the boil, swirl in the oil and add the pasta. Cook for 7-10 minutes or until tender yet firm. Rinse under cold running water and drain.
2 Put the pasta wheels in a large bowl and mix in the salami, spring onions, artichoke halves, black olives and tomato wedges.
3 Make the dressing: put all the ingredients in a screw-top jar, adding salt and pepper to taste, and shake well to mix.
4 Pour the dressing over the pasta mixture and toss until coated.
5 Arrange lettuce leaves around the edge of a serving dish, then spoon the pasta mixture into the centre.

Cook's Notes

TIME
Cooking the pasta wheels and preparing the salad take 20 minutes.

●565 calories/2375 kj per portion

VARIATIONS
Use drained canned asparagus instead of artichoke hearts.

Add chopped fresh herbs, such as coriander or tarragon, crumbled Feta cheese or 1 tablespoon tomato purée to vary the flavour. To turn this into a main course for four add sliced button mushrooms and cooked whole green beans.

Pasta with peppers and olives

SERVES 4

150 g/5 oz pasta bows
1 small red pepper, deseeded
1 small green pepper, deseeded
3 tablespoons olive oil
1 small onion, finely chopped
1 garlic clove, crushed (optional)
1 teaspoon dried oregano
100 g/4 oz black olives
salt and freshly ground black pepper

1 Cut the red and green peppers into thin 5 cm/2 inch lengths.
2 Heat the oil in a large saucepan, add the onion and garlic, if using, and fry gently for 5 minutes until soft and lightly coloured.
3 Add the peppers, oregano, salt and pepper and cook for a further 10 minutes, stirring from time to time.
4 Meanwhile, bring a large pan of salted water to the boil. Add the pasta and bring back to the boil, then lower the heat and simmer for about 10 minutes or until the pasta is just tender. Drain thoroughly (see Cook's tip).
5 Add the pasta and olives to the onion and peppers and mix well. Cook over low heat for a further 2 minutes, stirring occasionally. Transfer to a warmed serving dish and serve at once.

Cook's Notes

TIME
Preparation and cooking take about 30 minutes.

COOK'S TIP
Make sure the pasta bows are drained well; if the water is left lodged inside them the finished dish will be soggy and unappetizing.

VARIATIONS
The peppers and olives go very well with many other types of pasta. The dish can also be served cold as a salad to accompany a meat dish or as part of a buffet.

●270 calories/1125 kj per portion

Salmon kedgeree

SERVES 6

2 × 200 g/7 oz cans red salmon,
    drained and flaked
150 g/5 oz long-grain rice
salt
3 hard-boiled eggs
50 g/2 oz butter
freshly ground black pepper
150 ml/¼ pint soured cream or
    natural yoghurt
2 teaspoons curry powder
sweet paprika, to garnish

1 Cook the rice in plenty of boiling salted water until tender but not mushy (about 12 minutes). Drain in a colander and rinse thoroughly.
2 Place the rice in a warmed, buttered shallow serving dish, cover and keep warm in a low oven.
3 Chop 1 of the hard-boiled eggs and the white of the others, reserving the yolks.

4 Melt the butter in a saucepan over moderate heat. Add the salmon and the chopped egg, then shake the pan briefly over the heat to warm through. Season with salt and pepper. Add the salmon and egg to the rice.
5 In a small saucepan, warm through the soured cream or yoghurt over low heat, but do not allow to boil. Stir in the curry powder, beat with a wooden spoon until smooth, then pour over the rice mixture and fork it in lightly.
6 Press the reserved egg yolks through a sieve over the top of the kedgeree. Sprinkle with paprika to taste and serve at once.

Cook's Notes

 TIME
This dish takes 25 minutes to make.

 SERVING IDEAS
Serve with mango chutney. For a supper dish, serve with a green salad and ½ cucumber, thinly sliced and mixed with 150 g/5 oz natural yoghurt.

 COOK'S TIPS
When rinsing the rice, make a few holes in it with a spoon handle to drain it well and stop sticking.

Instead of keeping rice hot in the oven, an alternative way is to put the rice in a colander over a pan of hot water and cover with a clean, folded tea-towel.

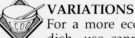 **VARIATIONS**
For a more economical dish, use canned tuna in place of salmon. For a traditional kedgeree, use 500 g/1 lb smoked haddock poached in milk to cover, with a bay leaf and a few black peppercorns added.

●465 calories/1950 kj per portion

Stuffed cabbage leaves

SERVES 6

12 large cabbage leaves
salt
1 tablespoon vegetable oil
1 small onion, finely chopped
4 rashers bacon, derinded and chopped
250 g/9 oz cooked rice (see Cook's tips)
100 g/4 oz full-fat soft cheese
2 tablespoons top of the milk
3 tomatoes, skinned and chopped
50 g/2 oz chopped mixed nuts
2 teaspoons sweet paprika
freshly ground black pepper
4 tablespoons chicken stock
margarine, for greasing

1 Heat the oven to 180C/350F/Gas 4 and grease a large ovenproof dish with margarine (see Cook's tips).
2 Bring a pan of salted water to the boil. Remove the tough rib at the base of the cabbage leaves and blanch them in the boiling water for 3 minutes. Drain carefully, refresh under cold running water, lay flat on a work surface and pat dry with absorbent paper.
3 Heat the oil in a small frying-pan, add the onion and bacon and fry gently for 5 minutes until the onion is soft and lightly coloured.
4 Using a slotted spoon, transfer the onion and bacon to a bowl and add the rice, cheese, milk, tomatoes, nuts and paprika. Season to taste with salt and black pepper.
5 Divide the mixture between the cabbage leaves, putting it in the centre of each leaf. Fold the 2 sides over the filling and then roll up each leaf to form a neat parcel.
6 Place the parcels, join side down, in the prepared dish. Season with salt and pepper, then pour over the chicken stock. Cover and bake in the oven for 1 hour. Serve at once.

Mixed fruit curry

SERVES 4

50 g/2 oz creamed coconut, broken into pieces (see Buying guide)
2 tablespoons curry paste (see Cook's tips)
150 ml/¼ pint soured cream
1 banana
½ honeydew melon, cut into 2.5 cm/1 inch cubes (see Buying guide)
100 g/4 oz each green and black grapes, halved and deseeded
1 orange, divided into segments
1 red dessert apple, cored (see Cook's tips)

1 Put the coconut, curry paste and soured cream into a large saucepan. Stir over low heat until the mixture is well blended.

2 Peel the banana, cut into 1 cm/½ inch slices and add to pan with the melon, grapes and orange. Cook gently, stirring, for 3-4 min-utes until the fruit is warm. Cut the apple into wedges, stir in and warm through. Spoon into a serving dish and serve at once.

Cook's Notes

TIME
20 minutes preparation, 5-6 minutes cooking.

SERVING IDEAS
Serve as a hot, but refreshing starter on a bed of plain boiled rice. The rice should be cooked *al dente* and so that each grain is separate.

BUYING GUIDE
Blocks of creamed coco-nut are available in packets from supermarkets and Indian food shops.
   Choose a melon that is not too ripe or it will break up.

VARIATIONS
Add 100 g/4 oz diced cooked chicken, ham or bacon to the fruit mixture to make a more substantial dish.

COOK'S TIPS
Use an apple corer to remove the core and leave the skin on to add colour.
   Use curry paste for this dish rather than curry powder. As the dish is only cooked for a few minutes, curry powder will give an uncooked flavour to the sauce.

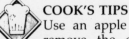

●280 calories/1150 kj per portion

Risotto alla Milanese

SERVES 6
50 g/2 oz butter
1 onion, very finely chopped
350 g/12 oz Italian rice (see Buying guide)
4 tablespoons dry white wine
1 L/2 pints hot chicken stock
¼ teaspoon powdered saffron (optional)
2 tablespoons finely grated Parmesan cheese
salt and freshly ground black pepper
extra Parmesan cheese, to serve

1 Melt half the butter in a heavy-based saucepan, add the onion and fry gently for 5 minutes until soft and lightly coloured.
2 Add the rice and continue to cook for 3 minutes, stirring constantly with a wooden spoon.

Cook's Notes

TIME
Preparation and cooking take 20-25 minutes.

WATCHPOINT
Take care not to 'mash' the rice at this stage.

BUYING GUIDE
Choose a medium-grain Italian rice rather than the more usual long-grain type. Arborio is ideal and can be found at Italian delicatessen stores or specialist grocers.

SERVING IDEAS
Besides serving as an unusual starter, *Risotto alla Milanese* is the traditional accompaniment to *Osso buco*. It is delicious served with any meat casserole or stew.

●455 calories/1900 kj per portion

3 Add the wine and continue to cook for 2 minutes, stirring.
4 Stir in hot stock, about 150 ml/ ¼ pint at a time, adding more as soon as each addition has been absorbed. If using saffron, dissolve the powder in 2 tablespoons of hot stock and add with the last addition. When all the stock has been absorbed, the rice should be moist and just creamy but not mushy.
5 When the grains of rice are tender but still firm, remove from the heat, add the remaining butter and sprinkle with the Parmesan cheese. Cover with a lid and leave to stand for 2 minutes.
6 Season well with salt and pepper and mix thoroughly with a fork. Top with extra Parmesan cheese.

Cannelloni
with tuna

SERVES 4

12 cannelloni tubes (see Buying
  guide)
50 g/2 oz margarine or butter
50 g/2 oz plain flour
500 ml/18 fl oz milk
200 g/7 oz can tuna, drained and
  flaked
100 g/4 oz frozen petits pois (see
  Buying guide)
salt and freshly ground black pepper
1 tablespoon tomato purée
generous pinch of sweet paprika
50 g/2 oz mature Cheddar cheese,
  finely grated
2 tablespoons grated Parmesan
  cheese
margarine or butter, for greasing

1 Heat the oven to 200C/400F/Gas 6.
Grease a shallow ovenproof dish.
2 Make the filling: melt the
margarine in a saucepan, sprinkle in
the flour and stir over low heat for
1-2 minutes until straw-coloured.
Remove from the heat and gradually
stir in 300 ml/½ pint of the milk.
Return to the heat and simmer,
stirring, until thick and smooth.
Remove from the heat.
3 Spoon half the sauce into a bowl,
then fold in the tuna and peas with
salt and pepper to taste.
4 With a small teaspoon, or a
forcing bag fitted with a large plain
nozzle, fill the cannelloni with the
filling mixture, pushing it well into
the tubes with your little finger.
5 Over low heat, gradually stir the
remaining milk into the reserved
sauce in the pan. Whisk vigorously
until smooth, then add the tomato
purée, sweet paprika and salt and
pepper to taste, then simmer for a
few minutes until thickened.
6 Cover the bottom of the prepared
dish with a little of the hot sauce,
then arrange the cannelloni on top,
separating each one with a little
sauce. Cover with the remaining
sauce. Mix the cheeses together,

then sprinkle over the top.
7 Bake in the oven for 30-35 minutes
until the sauce is bubbling at the

edges and the cannelloni are cooked
through. Serve hot, straight from
the dish.

Cook's Notes

TIME
Preparation takes 40
minutes, baking 30-35
minutes.

VARIATION
Use 100 g/4 oz cooked
ham or Italian salami,
finely chopped, instead of the
tuna.

BUYING GUIDE
Be sure to buy
cannelloni that do not
need pre-cooking. Instructions
are printed on the packet.
  Petits pois are the smallest

variety of frozen peas available,
and are, therefore, the most
suitable for filling cannelloni
tubes. If difficult to obtain, use
ordinary frozen peas.

DID YOU KNOW
Cannelloni is a favou-
rite dish in Italy; the
filling often includes veal, ham,
curd cheese or spinach.

SERVING IDEAS
Serve the cannelloni
with a mixed salad.

●530 calories/2225 kj per portion

Beef and spinach savoury

SERVES 4

500 g/1 lb lean minced beef
15 g/½ oz butter
1 tablespoon vegetable oil
1 large onion, chopped
225 g/8 oz tomatoes, chopped
1 tablespoon tomato purée
1 tablespoon mushroom ketchup
salt and freshly ground black pepper
100 g/4 oz vermicelli (see Buying guide)
2 × 300 g/10 oz packets frozen chopped spinach
1 large egg
1 tablespoon grated Parmesan cheese
½ teaspoon freshly grated nutmeg
150 ml/¼ pint soured cream
100 g/4 oz mushrooms, sliced
2 large tomatoes, sliced
100 g/4 oz Cheddar cheese, grated
margarine, for greasing

1 Heat the butter and oil in a large saucepan, add the onion and fry gently for 5 minutes, until soft and lightly coloured. Add the mince, turn the heat to high and fry for a further 5 minutes or until the meat has lost all its pinkness, stirring with a wooden spoon.

2 Add the tomatoes with their juice, tomato purée and mushroom ketchup. Stir well, bring to the boil and season with salt and pepper. Lower the heat, cover and simmer for about 30 minutes.

3 Meanwhile, bring a large saucepan of salted water to the boil, add the vermicelli and cook for about 5 minutes, until just tender. Cook the chopped spinach according to packet instructions.

4 Heat the oven to 180C/350F/Gas 4. Grease a shallow ovenproof dish.

5 Drain the vermicelli and cut it up roughly (see Preparation). Beat the egg and Parmesan cheese together in a bowl, and season with pepper and nutmeg. Add the chopped vermicelli and fork it through well. Spoon over base of dish.

6 Drain the spinach and put it into a bowl. Stir in the soured cream.

7 Spoon the beef and tomato mixture over the vermicelli. Arrange the sliced mushrooms on top and evenly spoon over the spinach and cream mixture.

8 Top with the tomato slices and sprinkle with the grated cheese. Cook in the oven for 20-30 minutes, until the cheese topping is melted and golden.

Cook's Notes

TIME
Preparation and cooking this dish take just over 1 hour.

BUYING GUIDE
Vermicelli, very thin pasta, cooks in half the time taken for spaghetti.

PREPARATION
To cut up vermicelli:

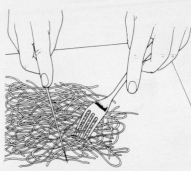

Use a knife and fork to cut up the vermicelli roughly on a wooden chopping board.

●635 calories/2650 kj per portion

Fishy noodle ring

SERVES 4

175 g/6 oz ribbon noodles (see Cook's tip)
salt
1 tablespoon vegetable oil
4 eggs, beaten
300 ml/½ pint milk
¼ teaspoon sweet paprika
25 g/1 oz butter, melted
watercress sprigs, to garnish

FISH SAUCE
500 g/1 lb cod fillets, skinned and cut into bite-sized pieces
2 tablespoons vegetable oil
1 large onion, chopped
750 g/1½ lb tomatoes, skinned and chopped
2 tablespoons tomato purée
2 teaspoons dried basil
½ teaspoon sugar
freshly ground black pepper

1 Heat the oven to 180C/350F/Gas 4.
2 Bring a large saucepan of salted water to the boil. Add the oil, then the noodles. Bring back to the boil, then lower the heat and simmer for 10-12 minutes until the noodles are tender but firm to the bite.
3 Meanwhile, whisk the eggs and milk together in a bowl, add the paprika and a pinch of salt.
4 Use half the melted butter to grease a 1.25 L/2 pint ring mould very generously. [!] Stir the remainder of the melted butter into the egg and milk mixture and pour into the buttered ring mould.
5 Drain the noodles, then spoon into the ring mould, arranging them evenly around it. Gently fork them into the liquid. Put the ring mould into a large roasting tin and half fill the tin with boiling water. Cook in oven for 40 minutes or until set.
6 Meanwhile, make the sauce: heat the oil in a saucepan, add the onion and fry gently for 5 minutes until soft and lightly coloured. Add the tomatoes and the purée and cook for about 20 minutes, until the sauce is thick. Stir in the basil and the sugar and then season with salt and pepper to taste.
7 Carefully lower the fish into the pan, stirring to coat the pieces in

sauce. Cook for another 5 minutes or until the fish flakes easily when tested with a fork.
8 To serve: run a knife around the edge of the mould, then invert a warmed serving plate on top. Hold the mould and plate firmly together and invert them, giving a sharp shake halfway round. Lift off the mould. Spoon some of the sauce into the middle and garnish with watercress. Spoon remainder of sauce into a warmed serving dish and hand separately.

Cook's Notes

 TIME
Preparation takes about 30 minutes. Cooking time is 40 minutes.

 COOK'S TIP
Use green or white tagliatelle-type noodles, or a mixture of both colours, for a pretty effect.

 SERVING IDEAS
This makes a satisfying, tasty main-course dish served with a green salad tossed in a generous dressing of oil and vinegar.

 VARIATIONS
The noodle ring may also be served cold: prepare to end of stage 5, then leave to cool completely. Omit stages 6 and 7, then unmould as in stage 8 and fill the ring with cold cooked fish pieces or prawns in a tomato-flavoured mayonnaise.

[!] WATCHPOINT
Butter the ring mould generously or the noodle ring will stick.

●530 calories/2200 kj per portion

Smoked haddock lasagne

SERVES 4

750 g/1½ lb smoked haddock fillets, skinned
2 bay leaves
pinch of ground cloves
1 onion, sliced
225 ml/8 fl oz water
150 ml/¼ pint dry white wine or cider
25 g/1 oz margarine or butter
2 tablespoons plain flour
100 g/4 oz Cheddar cheese, grated
freshly ground black pepper
350 g/12 oz tomatoes, skinned and sliced
200 g/7 oz lasagne (see Buying guide)
3 tablespoons fresh wholemeal breadcrumbs
1 tablespoon snipped chives
salt
margarine, for greasing
few extra bay leaves, to garnish (optional)

1 Heat the oven to 180C/350F/Gas 4. Grease an ovenproof dish.
2 Place the smoked haddock fillets in a large frying-pan and add the bay leaves, cloves and sliced onion. Pour the water and wine over the fish and bring to the boil. Lower the heat and simmer for 10 minutes, or until the fish flesh flakes easily when pierced with a sharp knife.
3 Using a fish slice, transfer the fish to a plate and leave to cool. Strain the cooking liquid into a measuring jug and measure out 300 ml/½ pint. Reserve the onion.
4 Flake the fish, discarding the skin and any bones.
5 Melt the margarine in a saucepan. Sprinkle in the flour and stir over low heat for 1-2 minutes, until straw-coloured. Gradually stir in the measured cooking liquid, then simmer, stirring, until thick and smooth. Stir all but 2 tablespoons of the cheese into the sauce, then add the flaked fish and reserved onion. Season to taste with pepper.
6 Place one-third of the fish mixture in the prepared dish and arrange half the tomato slices on top. Cover with half the lasagne. Repeat the layers, finishing with the remaining one-third of the fish mixture.
7 Mix together the breadcrumbs, remaining grated cheese and the chives in a bowl. Season to taste with salt and pepper and sprinkle the mixture evenly over the fish.
8 Cook in the oven for 30 minutes, until the lasagne is heated through and the topping is golden brown. Garnish with bay leaves, if liked.

Cook's Notes

TIME
Preparation takes about 30 minutes, cooking about 30 minutes.

BUYING GUIDE
Buy the type of lasagne that does not need pre-boiling but just requires heating through in the oven. It is widely available from supermarkets: check the packet carefully.

● 525 calories/2200 kj per portion

Beef and bean lasagne

SERVES 4

500 g/1 lb lean minced beef
2 tablespoons plus 1 teaspoon
   vegetable oil
2 onions, chopped
1 large green pepper, deseeded and
   chopped
2 tomatoes, skinned and chopped
1 tablespoon tomato purée
½ teaspoon dried oregano
1 beef stock cube, crumbled
½ tablespoon plain flour
salt and freshly ground black pepper
175-200 g/6-7 oz lasagne
420 g/15 oz can baked beans
75 g/3 oz Cheddar cheese, grated

1 Heat 2 tablespoons oil in a frying-pan. Add the onions and fry gently for 3-4 minutes until soft but not coloured. Add the green pepper and cook for a further 2-3 minutes, then add the minced beef, stirring with a wooden spoon to remove any lumps. Continue cooking for 3-4 minutes, stirring from time to time.
2 Add the tomatoes, tomato purée, oregano, stock cube, flour and salt and pepper to taste. Stir well to mix, then continue cooking gently for 20 minutes, stirring from time to time.
3 Meanwhile, add 1 teaspoon oil to a large pan of salted water and bring to the boil. Add the lasagne, a piece at a time (see Cook's tip) and boil rapidly, uncovered, for about 10 minutes or until just tender, stirring frequently. Drain, rinse then drain on absorbent paper.
4 Heat the oven to 200C/400F/Gas 6.
5 Spoon a thin layer of meat sauce into a deep ovenproof dish and cover with 2-3 pieces of lasagne. Spoon more of the meat sauce over one half and spoon some of the beans over the other half. Cover with another 2-3 pieces of lasagne. Spoon more meat sauce over the half where the beans were in the previous layer and more beans over the previous meat sauce layer. Continue layering and alternating the meat sauce and beans with the lasagne, ending with a layer of meat sauce and beans.
6 Sprinkle with the grated cheese, then bake in the oven for 20-25 minutes until the cheese is browned and the dish is bubbling.

Chicken Tetrazzini

SERVES 4

350 g/12 oz cooked boneless chicken, skin removed and cut into bite-sized pieces
salt
100 g/4 oz spaghetti
50 g/2 oz butter
100 g/4 oz whole button mushrooms
40 g/1½ oz plain flour
425 ml/¾ pint chicken stock
5 tablespoons dry white wine
150 ml/¼ pint double cream
pinch of freshly grated nutmeg
freshly ground black pepper
25 g/1 oz Parmesan cheese, grated

1 Heat the oven to 180C/350F/Gas 4.
2 Bring a large saucepan of salted water to the boil, add the spaghetti and cook until just tender, 10-12 minutes. Drain well. Return to the rinsed-out pan, cover with fresh cold water (see Cook's tip). Set aside.
3 Meanwhile, melt the butter in a saucepan, add the mushrooms and fry, stirring occasionally, for about 5 minutes until just tender. Remove with a slotted spoon and set aside.

4 Sprinkle the flour into the butter in the pan and stir over low heat for 1-2 minutes. Gradually stir in the stock and simmer, stirring, until the sauce is thickened and smooth. Remove from the heat and gradually stir in the wine and cream. Add the nutmeg and season to taste with salt and freshly ground black pepper.

5 Drain the spaghetti thoroughly, then stir it into the sauce with the fried mushrooms and chicken.
6 Pour the mixture into a shallow 1 L/2 pint ovenproof dish. Sprinkle the grated Parmesan cheese over the top and bake in the oven for about 30 minutes until golden. Serve hot, straight from the dish.

Cook's Notes

TIME
Preparation takes about 35 minutes, cooking about 30 minutes.

ECONOMY
The cream and stock may be replaced by a mixture of 300 ml/½ pint milk and 300 ml/½ pint stock. Replace the wine with cider and the Parmesan with 50 g/2 oz grated Cheddar cheese.

COOK'S TIP
The cooked spaghetti must be covered with cold water until it is required, to prevent the strands from sticking together.

●540 calories/2250 kj per portion

FREEZING
Use a rigid foil container but do not sprinkle the dish with the cheese. Cool quickly, then seal, label and freeze for up to 3 months. To serve: reheat from frozen in a 180C/350F/Gas 4 oven for about 1 hour. Stir the dish with a fork once or twice during cooking, and sprinkle with the cheese halfway through cooking time.

DID YOU KNOW
Chicken Tetrazzini is believed to have been created by the chef at Delmonico's, a famous New York restaurant, in honour of one of its best customers, Louisa Tetrazzini, who was extremely fond of spaghetti.

Pasta pie

SERVES 4
350 g/12 oz fresh tagliatelle (see Buying guide)
salt
1 teaspoon vegetable oil
25 g/1 oz margarine or butter
1 onion, roughly diced
1 tablespoon plain flour
300 ml/½ pint milk
250 g/9 oz cooked chicken, diced
200 g/7 oz can sweetcorn, drained
freshly ground black pepper
50 g/2 oz Cheddar cheese, grated
margarine, for greasing

1 Heat the oven to 200C/400F/Gas 6 and lightly grease a 1.5 L/2½ pint pie dish.
2 Bring a large pan of salted water to the boil, swirl in the oil and add the pasta. Bring back to the boil and then cook for 1 minute only. Drain well and leave to cool.
3 Meanwhile, melt the margarine in a saucepan, add the onion and fry for about 3-4 minutes until soft but not coloured. Sprinkle in the flour and stir over low heat for 1-2 minutes until straw-coloured.

Remove from heat and gradually stir in the milk. Return to the heat and simmer, stirring, until thick and smooth.
4 Stir in the chicken and sweetcorn and season with salt and pepper.
5 Using scissors, cut up the pasta.

Use two-thirds to line the prepared pie dish (see Preparation).
6 Pour the chicken mixture into the centre of the pasta. Place the rest of the pasta over the top. Sprinkle over the grated cheese and bake in the oven for about 25 minutes.

Cook's Notes

TIME
Preparation, including cooling time, is about 45 minutes. Cooking takes about 25 minutes.

! WATCHPOINT
Most pasta recipes advise rinsing pasta under cold running water to remove excess starch. Do not rinse the pasta in this recipe however, as the starch is needed to make it easier to line the prepared pie dish satisfactorily.

BUYING GUIDE
If fresh tagliatelle is not available, use 175 g/6 oz dried tagliatelle and cook for 7-8 minutes in stage 2.

● 630 calories/2650 kj per portion

PREPARATION
To line the pie dish with tagliatelle:

1 *Using scissors, cut the pasta into pieces the length of the pie dish.*

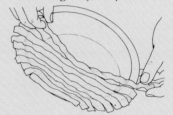

2 *Start at centre of dish and lay pasta until the whole dish is covered.*

Pasta with chicken liver sauce

SERVES 2-4

250 g/9 oz frozen chicken livers, defrosted and cut into small pieces (see Buying guide)
25 g/1 oz margarine
½ onion, thinly sliced
25-50 g/1-2 oz plain flour
50 ml/2 fl oz medium-dry sherry
175 g/6 oz mushrooms, sliced
150 ml/¼ pint chicken stock
½ teaspoon dried thyme
salt and freshly ground black pepper
350 g/12 oz pasta
15 g/½ oz butter
1 tablespoon top of the milk
little grated Parmesan (optional)
fresh thyme sprigs (optional)

1 Melt the margarine in a saucepan, add the onion and fry gently until soft but not coloured.
2 Toss the chicken livers in the flour to coat them. Add the chicken livers to the pan, raise the heat slightly and cook for 3-4 minutes until browned but still pink inside.
3 Add the sherry to the pan, stirring well to mix, then stir in the mushrooms. Stir in the chicken stock and bring to the boil. Add the thyme and season to taste with salt and pepper. Lower the heat, cover the pan and simmer gently for 12 minutes.
4 Meanwhile, cook the pasta according to packet directions until tender. Drain the cooked pasta and return to the rinsed-out pan with the butter and pepper to taste. Shake the pan vigorously to coat the pasta in the butter and pepper.
5 To serve: stir the top of the milk into the chicken liver sauce. Taste and adjust seasoning. Transfer the pasta to a warmed serving dish and spoon over the chicken liver sauce. Top with the Parmesan and thyme, if using. Serve at once.

Macaroni turkey

SERVES 4

750 g/1½ lb boneless turkey meat,
cut into 2.5 cm/1 inch cubes
(see Buying guide)
1 tablespoon vegetable oil
50 g/2 oz margarine or butter
1 large onion, chopped
2 celery stalks, chopped
2 teaspoons plain flour
300 g/10 oz can condensed cream of
chicken soup
300 ml/½ pint chicken stock
salt and freshly ground black pepper
2 teaspoons French mustard
175 g/6 oz wholewheat macaroni
250 g/9 oz mushrooms, sliced
2 tablespoons chopped parsley
50 g/2 oz fresh white breadcrumbs
tomato slices, to garnish

1 Heat oil and half the margarine in a large frying-pan. Add the onion and celery and fry gently for 1-2 minutes. Add the turkey and fry briskly for a further 3-4 minutes, stirring often, to brown on all sides.
2 Sprinkle the flour into the frying-pan and stir over low heat for 1-2 minutes. Remove from the heat and stir in the soup and the chicken stock. Return to heat and bring to the boil, stirring. Season to taste. Lower the heat, add the mustard and simmer for 20 minutes.
3 Heat the oven to 200C/400F/Gas 6.
4 Meanwhile, bring a large pan of salted water to the boil and cook the macaroni for 10 minutes. Drain well. Melt the remaining margarine in the rinsed-out pan, add the macaroni and stir it well to coat thoroughly.
5 Spoon the macaroni over the base of a large ovenproof dish.
6 Stir the sliced mushrooms into the turkey mixture and spoon over macaroni. Sprinkle with the parsley and breadcrumbs and bake for 20 minutes. Serve hot, straight from the dish, garnished with tomato slices.

Cook's Notes

TIME
Preparation takes about 20 minutes, cooking time about 40 minutes.

BUYING GUIDE
Boneless light and dark turkey meat, cut into chunks, is available in casserole packs from the chilling and freezer cabinets of large supermarkets and freezer centres. Defrost frozen turkey meat before using in this recipe.

● 600 calories/2500 kj per portion

Spicy sausage macaroni

SERVES 4-6
500 g/1 lb chorizo sausages (see
    Buying guide)
salt
350 g/12 oz short-cut macaroni
15 g/½ oz lard
1 small onion, finely chopped
2 × 250 g/9 oz cans tomato or
    mushroom spaghetti sauce
1 teaspoon dried oregano (optional)
freshly ground black pepper
175 g/6 oz mild Cheddar cheese,
    grated
margarine, for greasing

1 Bring a large saucepan of salted water to the boil. Meanwhile, skin the sausages.

2 Heat the oven to 180C/350F/Gas 4. Drop the macaroni into the boiling water and cook according to packet instructions until just tender. [!] Drain thoroughly.

3 While the macaroni is cooking, melt the lard in a large frying-pan, add the sausages and fry, turning, until brown on all sides. Remove the sausages from the pan, drain on absorbent paper and set aside.

4 Add the onion to the pan and fry gently, stirring often, until it is soft and golden. Remove from the pan with a slotted spoon and pour away the fat left in the pan.

5 Cut the sausages into 1 cm/½ inch pieces. Return to the pan with the onion, spaghetti sauce and oregano, if using. Season carefully with salt and pepper. Bring the contents of the pan to simmering point.

6 Lightly grease a 1.75 L/3 pint casserole. Form separate layers of macaroni, sausage and sauce, and one-third of the cheese. Repeat these layers once, then finish with a layer of macaroni. Sprinkle the top with the remaining one-third of the grated cheese, making sure all the macaroni is covered. [!]

7 Bake in the oven for about 30 minutes, until the topping is golden and the macaroni heated through.

Cook's Notes

TIME
Preparation, including boiling the pasta, takes about 20 minutes. Cooking in the oven takes about 30 minutes.

BUYING GUIDE
Chorizos are sold cooked and uncooked in delicatessens: make sure you buy the uncooked variety for this dish.

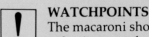
WATCHPOINTS
The macaroni should be only just tender after boiling, so it does not become mushy when heated through in the oven.

It should be completely covered with cheese, so that the top layer does not become hard or brittle.

●850 calories/3575 kj per portion

Salmon in puff pastry

SERVES 4

215 g/7½ oz can red salmon (see Buying guide), drained and flaked, skin and bones discarded
50 g/2 oz long-grain rice
salt
2 hard-boiled eggs, chopped
2 tablespoons chopped parsley or snipped chives
50 g/2 oz margarine or butter, melted
2 tablespoons tomato ketchup
freshly ground black pepper
375 g/13 oz frozen puff pastry, defrosted
1 small egg, beaten

1 Heat the oven to 220C/425F/Gas 7.
2 Rinse the rice thoroughly under cold running water, then cook in a saucepan of boiling salted water for 12 minutes. Drain and rinse again under cold running water to separate the grains.
3 Put the salmon in a large bowl with the rice, hard-boiled eggs, parsley, melted margarine, tomato ketchup and salt and pepper to taste. Fold gently to mix, taking care not to break up the pieces of salmon and egg.
4 Roll out the pastry on a floured surface to a rectangle about 35 × 25 cm/14 × 10 inches. Transfer to a dampened baking sheet.
5 Place the salmon and rice mixture in the centre of the pastry, spreading it out evenly. Dampen the edges of the pastry and press them together over the top of the filling. Crimp the edges and make 3-4 cuts each side.
6 Brush the pastry all over with beaten egg, then bake in the oven for about 40 minutes until golden brown. [!] Serve hot or cold.

Cook's Notes

TIME
Preparation about 20 minutes, including cooking the rice and hard-boiling the eggs. Cooking takes about 40 minutes.

BUYING GUIDE
Red, rather than pink salmon is recommended for this pie because of its finer flavour and colour.

WATCHPOINT
If the pastry browns too quickly, cover with foil.

DID YOU KNOW
This is an easy version of a delicious Russian fish pie, called *kulibyaka*.

●630 calories/2625 kj per portion

Mock paella

SERVES 6

3 kabanos sausages, chopped into
   1 cm/½ inch lengths
340 g/11 oz can luncheon meat, cut
   into 1 cm/½ inch dice
2 tablespoons vegetable oil
1 large onion, chopped
1 large red pepper, deseeded and
   chopped
2 cloves garlic, crushed (optional)
175 g/6 oz smoked streaky bacon
   rashers, rinds removed and
   chopped
3 tomatoes, skinned and chopped
1 teaspoon ground turmeric
350 g/12 oz long-grain rice, rinsed
225 g/8 oz frozen peas
600-700 ml/1-1¼ pints chicken
   stock
2 bay leaves
salt and freshly ground black pepper
198 g/7 oz can shrimps, drained
lemon wedges, to garnish

1 Heat the oil in a large frying-pan, add the onion, red pepper and garlic, if using, and fry gently for 5 minutes until the onion is soft and lightly coloured. Add the bacon and continue to cook for 3 minutes, then add the tomatoes and cook for a further 5 minutes.

2 Add the chopped kabanos and luncheon meat and continue to cook, stirring, for 2 minutes.

3 Stir in the turmeric, rice and frozen peas. Add about 600 ml/1 pint of chicken stock, stir well and add the bay leaves. Season with salt and pepper to taste and simmer gently for 20-25 minutes, stirring occasionally until the rice is tender and the liquid has been absorbed. Stir in the remaining stock, a little at a time, during cooking if the paella begins to look dry and the rice is not quite cooked.

4 Add the shrimps and stir until they are heated through. Discard the bay leaves, transfer the paella to a warmed serving dish and serve at once, garnished with lemon wedges.

Cook's Notes

TIME
15 minutes preparation,
35-40 minutes cooking.

SERVING IDEAS
The dish is a meal in itself, but serve with a green salad, if liked.

VARIATIONS
The ingredients can be varied according to taste and what stores you have to hand. For instance, try using left-over chicken or pork instead of the luncheon meat. Add a jar of drained mussels if your purse can stretch to it. A small can of sweetcorn makes an interesting addition, too.

●705 calories/2950 kj per portion

Pork and mushroom risotto

SERVES 4

350 g/12 oz pork fillet, cut into 2.5 cm/1 inch cubes
100 g/4 oz streaky bacon rashers, derinded and cut into 1 cm/½ inch dice
50 g/2 oz margarine or butter
2 onions, chopped
1 clove garlic, crushed (optional)
1 green pepper, deseeded and thinly sliced
1 red pepper, deseeded and thinly sliced
300 g/11 oz long-grain rice
about 850 ml/1½ pints hot chicken stock
3 large tomatoes, skinned and chopped
salt and freshly ground black pepper
100 g/4 oz mushrooms, thinly sliced
2 tablespoons chopped fresh parsley
50 g/2 oz Parmesan cheese, grated

1 Fry the bacon in a large frying-pan with a lid over moderate heat for 3-4 minutes until the fat runs.

Remove the bacon from the pan with a slotted spoon and set aside.
2 Lower heat and melt 40 g/1½ oz of the margarine in the pan. Add the onions and garlic, if using, and fry gently for 5 minutes until soft and lightly coloured. Add the peppers to the pan and fry, stirring occasionally, for 2 minutes. Remove the vegetables with a slotted spoon and reserve with the bacon.
3 Add the cubes of pork to the pan and fry, turning often, for 6-8 minutes until evenly browned on all sides.
4 Add the rice to the pan and stir to coat all the grains with fat. Stir in the chicken stock. Return the bacon, onions and peppers to the pan, add the tomatoes and season with salt and pepper to taste. Bring to the boil, stir well to mix, then lower the heat, cover and simmer very gently for 40 minutes. [!]
5 Melt the remaining margarine in a small saucepan, add the mushrooms and fry for 1-2 minutes, stirring occasionally.
6 Stir the mushrooms into the risotto. Taste the rice grains—they should be just tender, but not soft. If necessary, cook for a few minutes longer, adding a little more hot stock if needed. Taste and adjust seasoning if necessary.
7 Turn the risotto into a warmed serving dish and sprinkle with the parsley and cheese. Serve at once.

Lamb pilaff

SERVES 4

250 g/9 oz cooked lean lamb, cut
   into strips (see Variations)
250 g/9 oz Basmati or
   long-grain rice
25 g/1 oz butter
300 ml/½ pint boiling water
2 tablespoons vegetable oil
1 onion, finely chopped
2 teaspoons curry powder
½ teaspoon turmeric powder
4 tablespoons currants
4 tablespoons flaked almonds
2 tomatoes, skinned and chopped
finely grated zest of ½ lemon
1 tablespoon chopped fresh mint
salt and freshly ground black pepper
mint leaves, lemon slices and silver
   leaf, to garnish (see Did you
   know)

Cook's Notes

 TIME
Preparation and cook-
ing this dish take about
40 minutes.

 DID YOU KNOW
Silver leaf, or *varak*,
which is available from
Indian food shops, is an edible garnish used in Indian cooking, often in the creamier dishes.

 VARIATIONS
Any cooked meat or
poultry may be used
and herbs varied accordingly.

●530 calories/2225 kj per portion

1 Rinse the rice thoroughly under cold running water, drain, then place in a large heavy-based sauce-pan with the butter. Pour in the boiling water, bring back to the boil, then cover with a tight-fitting lid and simmer very gently for about 10 minutes until the water is absorbed and the rice is just tender.

2 Heat the oil in a large frying-pan, add the onion, curry powder and turmeric and then fry gently for 5 minutes until the onion is soft. Add the rice and cook the mixture for a further 5 minutes, stirring constantly.

3 Add the lamb, currants and almonds and cook gently for a further 5 minutes, stirring constant-ly. Stir in the tomatoes, lemon zest and mint and cook for a further 2 minutes. Season to taste.

4 Pile the lamb pilaff on to a warmed serving dish, garnish with mint leaves, lemon slices and silver leaf. Serve at once.

Mexican beef layer

SERVES 4

250 g/9 oz lean minced beef
1 tablespoon vegetable oil
2 onions, finely chopped
4 streaky bacon rashers, derinded and finely chopped
1 clove garlic, crushed (optional)
1 bay leaf
2 teaspoons tomato purée
1 tablespoon tomato ketchup
1 tablespoon sultanas
1 tablespoon Demerara sugar
½ teaspoon chilli powder
150 ml/¼ pint beef stock
salt
175 g/6 oz Italian risotto rice
1 green pepper, deseeded and finely chopped
425 g/15 oz can red kidney beans, drained
freshly ground black pepper
margarine, for greasing
1 small avocado, to garnish
300 ml/½ pint thick home-made tomato sauce, to serve

1 Heat the oil in a large saucepan, add the chopped onion and the chopped bacon and fry gently for 5 minutes, until the onion is soft and lightly coloured. With a slotted spoon, transfer the onion and bacon to a plate and set aside.

2 Add the minced beef to the pan and fry over brisk heat for a few minutes until the meat is evenly browned, stirring with a wooden spoon to remove any lumps.

3 Return the onion and bacon to the pan with the garlic, if using, the bay leaf, tomato purée, tomato ketchup, sultanas, sugar, chilli powder and stock. Cover the pan, bring almost to the boil then lower heat and cook very gently for about 30 minutes, stirring occasionally.

4 Meanwhile, bring a large saucepan of salted water to the boil, add the rice and cook for 10 minutes, then add the green pepper and cook for a further 5 minutes or until the rice is tender. Drain.

5 Remove the meat mixture from the heat. Liberally grease a 1 L/2 pint pudding basin. Spoon a layer of rice into the basin, followed by a layer of meat mixture, then a layer of beans. Repeat these layers once more, then top with a final layer of rice. Cover the basin with foil and place in a large saucepan. Pour in boiling water to come halfway up the sides of the basin, cover and simmer the beef layer for 40 minutes.

6 Remove the pudding basin from the saucepan, using oven gloves. Cool slightly, remove the foil and run a knife around the basin. Insert a warmed serving plate on top and carefully turn out the beef layer.

7 Peel and slice the avocado. Top the beef layer with avocado slices and serve at once, with tomato sauce handed separately.

Kidney and rice ring

SERVES 6
**750 g/1½ lb lamb kidneys, cores
   removed, quartered**
50 g/2 oz butter
1 large onion, thinly sliced
**100 g/4 oz button mushrooms,
   quartered**
4 streaky bacon rashers, chopped
2-3 tablespoons plain flour
150 ml/¼ pint chicken stock
1-2 tablespoons lemon juice
1 teaspoon tomato purée
150 ml/¼ pint soured cream
salt and freshly ground black pepper
sweet paprika, to finish
celery leaves, to garnish

RICE RING
50 g/2 oz butter
1 large onion, chopped
1 teaspoon ground turmeric
250 g/9 oz long-grain rice
700 ml/1¼ pints chicken stock
1 bay leaf
butter, for greasing

1 Heat the oven to 180C/350F/Gas 4. Grease a 1L/2 pint ring mould well.
2 Prepare the rice ring: melt half the butter in a flameproof casserole, add the onion and fry gently for 5 minutes until it is soft and lightly coloured. Stir in the turmeric, then add rice. Stir to coat all the grains.
3 Pour the 700 ml/1¼ pints chicken stock on to the rice, then add the bay leaf and stir well. Bring to the boil, cover and cook in the oven for 20-30 minutes until the rice is tender and all the stock has been absorbed. Stir in the remaining butter.
4 Pack the cooked rice into the prepared ring mould, pressing it down well. Cover with foil and cook in the oven for 10 minutes.
5 Meanwhile, prepare the kidney filling: melt the butter in a large frying-pan, add the onion and mushrooms and fry gently for 5 minutes until the onion is soft and lightly coloured. Transfer the onion and the mushrooms to a plate with a slotted spoon.
6 Add the kidneys and bacon to the pan and fry over moderate heat, stirring frequently, for about 5 minutes until cooked through.

7 Sprinkle in the flour and stir over low heat for 1-2 minutes then gradually stir in the stock, lemon juice to taste and the tomato purée. Simmer, stirring, until the sauce is thick and smooth.
8 Carefully turn the rice mould out on to a warmed serving dish.
9 Stir the onion, mushrooms and soured cream into the kidney mixture. Season to taste. Warm through without boiling and spoon into the centre of the rice ring. Sprinkle with paprika, garnish dish with celery leaves and serve.

Cook's Notes

TIME
Preparation takes about 15 minutes. Cooking takes about 30 minutes, finishing about 5 minutes.

SERVING IDEAS
Serve with hot sliced beetroot lightly cooked in creamy horseradish sauce.

●520 calories/2175 kj per portion

Ginger Chicken

SERVES 4

3 chicken breast joints, boned, each
   weighing about 200 g/7 oz, cut
   into strips 5 cm/2 inches long and
   1 cm/½ inch wide
25 g/1 oz margarine or butter
1 tablespoon vegetable oil
1 large onion, roughly chopped
1 clove garlic, crushed (optional)
3 tablespoons ginger preserve
2 tablespoons soy sauce
1 tablespoon lemon juice
freshly ground black pepper

SWEETCORN RICE
175 g/6 oz long-grain rice
salt
225 g/8 oz frozen sweetcorn
25 g/1 oz walnut pieces, roughly
   chopped

1 Heat the margarine and oil in a frying-pan or wok and add the chicken strips, onion and garlic, if using. Cook over moderate heat, stirring occasionally, for 15 minutes until the chicken is golden and cooked through.

2 Meanwhile, cook the rice: bring a large pan of salted water to the boil, add the rice, bring back to the boil and simmer for 5 minutes. Add the sweetcorn and continue cooking for 10 minutes until the rice is tender.

3 Stir the preserve, soy sauce and lemon juice into the chicken with pepper to taste. [!] Continue cooking for a further 5 minutes until the ingredients are well blended.

4 Drain the rice mixture and stir in the chopped walnuts. Transfer to a warmed serving dish and spoon the chicken mixture into the centre. Serve at once (see Serving ideas).

Cook's Notes

TIME
Preparation and cooking of this dish take about 40 minutes.

WATCHPOINT
Salt should not be necessary, as the soy sauce will add enough salt.

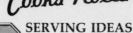

SERVING IDEAS
This quantity of chicken is enough to make a light meal with the sweetcorn rice accompaniment. For a more substantial main course dish, use 4 chicken breasts.

Instead of serving with the rice, serve with pasta shapes.

VARIATIONS
Chunky orange marmalade can be substituted for the ginger preserve. Use a 300 g/11 oz can sweetcorn instead of frozen. Heat gently drain and stir into rice.

●545 calories/2275 kj per portion

Spiced rice chicken

SERVES 4

350 g/12 oz boneless chicken
    breasts, skinned and cut into 2.5
    cm/1 inch pieces
50 g/2 oz margarine or butter
1 tablespoon vegetable oil
1 onion, chopped
1 clove garlic, crushed (optional)
1 teaspoon ground cumin
1 teaspoon ground coriander
½ teaspoon ground ginger
½ teaspoon ground turmeric
150 ml/¼ pint orange juice
425 ml/¾ pint chicken stock
175 g/6 oz long-grain rice
50 g/2 oz seedless raisins
50 g/2 oz salted peanuts

1 Heat the oven to 180C/350F/Gas 4.
2 Heat the margarine and oil in a
frying-pan, add the chicken pieces
and fry over moderate heat until
browned on all sides. With a slotted
spoon, transfer the chicken to an
ovenproof serving dish.
3 Add the onion and garlic, if
using, to the frying-pan and fry
gently for 5 minutes until the onion
is soft and lightly coloured. Stir in
the spices, orange juice, chicken
stock and the rice and bring to the
boil.
4 Pour the mixture over the chicken
and cook in the oven for about 45
minutes until the chicken and rice
are tender. Stir in the raisins and
peanuts and serve at once, straight
from the dish.

Cook's Notes

TIME
This very quick dish
takes 15 minutes to pre-
pare, and about 45 minutes
cooking in the oven.

VARIATIONS
Use turkey breasts in-
stead of chicken, and
brown rice instead of long-
grain. If using brown rice, allow
about 15 minutes longer in the
oven.

●500 calories/2075 kj per portion

PARTY DISHES

Nasi goreng

Every rice-growing country develops its own special savoury rice dishes. This one, *Nasi Goreng*, which means literally fried rice, is a great favourite from Indonesia.

SERVES 4-6
350 g/12 oz long-grain rice
450 ml/16 fl oz water
1 tablespoon vegetable oil
15 g/½ oz butter
3 shallots, finely sliced
2 red chillis, finely chopped, or
  ½ teaspoon chilli powder
1 clove garlic, crushed (optional)
100 g/4 oz streaky bacon rashers or
  boneless chicken breast, diced
100 g/4 oz button mushrooms,
  finely sliced
1 teaspoon sweet paprika
1 tablespoon light soy sauce (see
  Buying guide)
2 teaspoons tomato purée or
  ketchup

TO GARNISH
cucumber slices
tomato slices
fried onions (see Buying guide)
  or spring onion tops
prawn crackers

1 Rinse the rice thoroughly under cold running water and put it in a large, heavy-based saucepan with a close-fitting lid. Pour in the water (see Cook's tips), bring to the boil, then simmer, uncovered, for 10-15 minutes, until all the water is absorbed. Stir once, then cover the pan tightly ! and cook for a further 10 minutes over the lowest possible heat (see Cook's tips).
2 Spoon the rice on to a large plate, fork it through to separate grains and leave to cool for 2 hours. !
3 Heat the oil and butter in a wok or large frying-pan. Add the shallots, chillis and garlic, if using, and fry over moderate heat, stirring, for 1-2 minutes. Add the bacon and mushrooms and fry, stirring, for a further 2 minutes. Add the paprika, soy sauce and tomato purée and cook, stirring, for 1 minute, until bacon and mushrooms are tender.
4 Add the rice and stir well over gentle heat until heated through. Add salt and a little more soy sauce to taste. Pile the mixture on to a warmed serving dish and garnish with cucumber, tomato, fried or spring onions and prawn crackers.

Cook's Notes

 TIME
Preparation takes about 10 minutes. Cooking the rice takes 20-25 minutes. Allow 2 hours cooling time for the rice. Cooking then takes about 5 minutes.

 COOK'S TIPS
Cook the rice in unsalted water; do not add salt until fully cooked.
If cooking on gas, cook the rice for the final 10 minutes with a heat-dispensing mat underneath the pan. Some of the rice will stick to the pan, but it comes away after soaking.

! WATCHPOINTS
Be sure to cover the pan very tightly, so that none of the steam can escape.
The rice for *nasi goreng* needs to be cold but freshly cooked: do not leave it overnight.

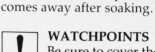 **BUYING GUIDE**
Use light soy sauce for *nasi goreng*: rich soy sauce is much darker, through longer cooking and a higher caramel content, and would make the dish an unattractive colour. Light and rich soy sauce are used in Chinese cooking rather like white and red wine in European cuisine: the light variety goes with vegetable, chicken and fish dishes; the rich variety goes with dark meats.
Ready-cooked, crisp-fried onions are available in tubs from large supermarkets: they are delicious and ideal for this recipe.

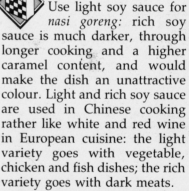 **SERVING IDEAS**
In Indonesia, *nasi goreng* is served at any time of day as a light meal in itself. Sometimes an omelette is cut into narrow strips and laid on top of it, other times it is topped with a fried egg for each person.
Nasi goreng may also accompany a main-course dish such as beef or chicken *saté*.

●480 calories/2000 kj per portion

Beef cannelloni

SERVES 4-6

16 cannelloni tubes (see Buying guide)
50 g/2 oz butter
50 g/2 oz Parmesan cheese, grated
extra butter, for greasing

FILLING
500 g/1 lb minced beef
50 g/2 oz butter
1 carrot, finely chopped
½ onion, finely chopped
1 clove garlic, crushed
1 celery stalk, finely chopped
salt and freshly ground black pepper
1 tablespoon plain flour
125 ml/4 fl oz dry white wine
400 g/14 oz can tomatoes, drained and roughly chopped
½ teaspoon dried oregano
1 tablespoon finely chopped fresh parsley

SAUCE
50 g/2 oz butter
50 g/2 oz plain flour
500 ml/18 fl oz milk
freshly grated nutmeg

1 Make the filling: melt the butter in a saucepan, add the carrot, onion, garlic, and celery and fry gently for 10 minutes until the onion is browned.

2 Add the minced beef, increase the heat to moderate and fry until the meat is evenly browned, stirring with a wooden spoon to remove any lumps. Season to taste with salt and pepper.

3 Lower the heat, then sprinkle in the flour and stir for 2 minutes. Remove from the heat and gradually stir in the wine, tomatoes and oregano.

4 Return to the heat, bring to the boil, then simmer for 20-25 minutes, stirring occasionally, until the meat is cooked and the sauce has thickened. Remove from the heat, stir in the parsley, then taste and adjust seasoning. Leave to cool.

5 Heat the oven to 200C/400F/Gas 6 and meanwhile grease a large ovenproof dish.

6 Make the sauce: melt the butter in a saucepan, sprinkle in the flour and stir over low heat for 1-2 minutes until straw-coloured. Remove from the heat and gradually stir in the milk. Return to the heat and simmer, stirring, until thick and smooth. Season with salt and pepper to taste and a generous sprinkling of nutmeg. Remove from the heat.

7 With a small teaspoon, stuff the cannelloni with the filling mixture. Cover the bottom of the dish with a little of the white sauce, then arrange the filled cannelloni in a single row in the dish, separating each one with a little sauce. Cover with the remaining sauce, then dot with the butter and sprinkle with the Parmesan cheese. ❄

8 Bake in the oven for 20 minutes, then cover with foil and continue to cook for a further 20 minutes or until the cannelloni are cooked through. Serve at once while still piping hot.

Cook's Notes

TIME
50 minutes preparation, including assembling, and about 40 minutes cooking in the oven.

BUYING GUIDE
Buy cannelloni that does not need pre-cooking. Instructions are printed on the packet.

FREEZING
Freeze before baking in the oven. Cool, seal, label and freeze for up to 3 months. To serve: cook from frozen in the oven for about 1 hour or until heated right through.

●690 calories/2905 kj per portion

Chicken timballo

SERVES 4-6

500 g/1 lb short-cut macaroni
350 g/12 oz uncooked chicken meat,
   finely chopped
75 g/3 oz butter
½ carrot, finely chopped
½ onion, finely chopped
¼ teaspoon dried thyme
1 celery stalk, finely chopped
100 g/4 oz lean bacon rashers, rinds
   removed and cut into thin strips
50 g/2 oz button mushrooms, sliced
125 ml/4 fl oz dry white wine
salt and freshly ground black pepper
40 g/1½ oz fine breadcrumbs,
   toasted
100 g/4 oz Parmesan cheese, grated

SAUCE
50 g/2 oz butter
50 g/2 oz plain flour
400 ml/14 fl oz milk
freshly grated nutmeg

TO GARNISH
tomato slices
sprigs of watercress

1 Melt 50 g/2 oz butter in a large saucepan, add the carrot, onion, thyme and celery and fry gently for 10 minutes.
2 Add the bacon and mushrooms to the pan and continue to fry for 2 minutes, stirring constantly.
3 Add the chicken to the pan and fry over moderate heat until evenly browned. Stir in the wine and season to taste with salt and pepper. Cover and cook gently for 25 minutes until the chicken is tender.
4 Meanwhile, cook the macaroni: bring a large pan of salted water to the boil. Add the macaroni, bring back to the boil and simmer for about 10 minutes, stirring occasionally, until tender yet firm.
5 Meanwhile, make the sauce: melt butter in a saucepan, sprinkle in the flour and stir over low heat for 1-2 minutes until straw-coloured. Remove from the heat and gradually stir in the milk. Return to the heat and simmer, stirring, until thick and smooth. Season with salt and pepper and a generous sprinkling of nutmeg. Remove from the heat.
6 Drain the macaroni and set aside. Heat the oven to 200C/400F/Gas 6. Grease a 3 L/5¼ pint casserole dish with the remaining butter and coat the base and sides with two-thirds of the breadcrumbs.
7 Mix the chicken mixture with the macaroni, sauce and Parmesan cheese and turn into the lined dish. Sprinkle the remaining breadcrumbs over the top. ✳ Cover and cook in the oven for 20 minutes. Turn off the heat and leave in the oven for a further 5 minutes. To serve: run a round-bladed knife around the edge of the timballo, then turn out on to a serving plate and garnish with tomato and watercress.

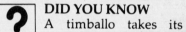

Seafood macaroni bake

SERVES 4

350 g/12 oz fresh or frozen haddock fillets, skinned (see Cook's tips)
600 ml/1 pint milk
1 lemon (see Preparation)
1 bay leaf
3 whole black peppercorns
salt
50 g/2 oz margarine or butter
250 g/9 oz mushrooms, thinly sliced
250 g/9 oz short-cut macaroni, boiled, drained and rinsed (see Watchpoint)
150 g/5 oz jar mussels, drained
40 g/1½ oz plain flour
250 g/9 oz peeled prawns (see Cook's tips)
pinch of freshly grated nutmeg
freshly ground black pepper
margarine, for greasing
extra lemon slices and unpeeled fresh prawns, to garnish (optional)

1 Put the haddock in a large frying-pan with a lid and pour in enough of the milk to just cover. Add 2 slices of lemon, the bay leaf, peppercorns and a good pinch of salt.

Bring gradually to the boil, then cover and turn off the heat under the pan. Leave to stand for 5 minutes, then remove the haddock with a fish slice. Flake the flesh into 4 cm/1½ inch pieces, discarding any bones. Strain all the cooking liquid and reserve.

2 Melt 15 g/½ oz margarine in the rinsed-out frying-pan, add the sliced mushrooms and fry for 2-3 minutes. Stir in the lemon juice and remove from heat.

3 Heat the oven to 180C/350F/Gas 4.

4 Put the macaroni into a greased large ovenproof dish with the haddock, mushrooms and mussels. Stir carefully to mix, without breaking up the fish.

5 Melt the remaining margarine in a saucepan, sprinkle in the flour and stir over low heat for 1-2 minutes until straw-coloured. Remove from the heat and gradually stir in rest of milk and reserved cooking liquid. Return to the heat and simmer, stirring, until thick and smooth. Remove from heat, stir in the prawns, nutmeg and salt and pepper to taste, then pour evenly over macaroni and fish mixture. Cook in the oven for 20 minutes.

6 Garnish with lemon slices and unpeeled prawns, if liked, and serve hot, straight from the dish.

Cook's Notes

 TIME
Preparation, 30 minutes; cooking in the oven, 20 minutes.

 COOK'S TIPS
If using frozen haddock, there is no need to defrost before using: after bringing to the boil in stage 1, simmer for a few minutes until thoroughly defrosted before turning off heat under pan.

If using frozen prawns, there is no need to defrost them before adding to the sauce.

 PREPARATION
Squeeze the juice from one-half of the lemon and slice the other half.

! **WATCHPOINT**
Take care not to overcook the macaroni at this stage, as it will continue cooking in the oven. Rinsing it under cold running water after it has been boiled prevents it from sticking together.

●610 calories/2550 kj per portion

Peppered pork and prawns

SERVES 4

250 g/9 oz pork fillet, trimmed of
   excess fat, cut into 1 cm/
   ½ inch cubes
2 tablespoons olive oil
1 red, 1 green and 1 yellow pepper,
   deseeded and cut into 5 cm ×
   5 mm/2 × ¼ inch strips (see
   Buying guide)
1 large onion, chopped
100 g/4 oz frozen peeled prawns,
   defrosted
1 tablespoon dry sherry
1 teaspoon Tabasco
freshly ground black pepper

SPICY NOODLES
175 g/6 oz ribbon noodles
salt
1 teaspoon vegetable oil
½ teaspoon ground turmeric
¼ teaspoon ground coriander
¼ teaspoon ground cumin

Cook's Notes

TIME
20 minutes preparation
plus about 15 minutes
cooking time.

ECONOMY
Use spare-rib pork
chops instead of pork
fillet, but allow 350 g/12 oz as
this cut of pork usually has
some bone and more fat. Shoulder of pork steaks can also be
used for this recipe.

VARIATIONS
Thinly sliced topside or
rump steak can be used
instead of pork. Or, use cooked
meat such as roast pork or
chicken and add with the
prawns when the peppers are
cooked. Allow another minute
for heating.

BUYING GUIDE
If yellow peppers are
difficult to buy, use 2
green peppers and 1 red one.

● 375 calories/1575 kj per portion

1 Cook the noodles: bring a large
pan of salted water to the boil, swirl
in the oil, then add the noodles and
the spices. Bring back to the boil
and cook for 7-10 minutes until the
ribbon noodles are tender yet still
firm to the bite.
2 Meanwhile, heat the oil in a
frying-pan, add peppers and onion
and cook for 3 minutes, stirring.

3 Add the pork cubes and cook for
a further 8 minutes, stirring.
4 Stir in the prawns, sherry and
Tabasco, season to taste with salt
and pepper and cook for 2 minutes.
5 Drain the noodles thoroughly
and arrange on 4 warmed serving
plates or in individual bowls. Spoon
over the pork and prawn mixture
and serve at once.

Lamb and pasta medley

SERVES 4

500 g/1 lb minced raw lamb
2 tablespoons olive oil
1 onion, chopped
1 green pepper, deseeded and
chopped
2 courgettes, finely chopped
400 g/14 oz can tomatoes
300 ml/½ pint water
250 g/9 oz pasta shapes
½ teaspoon dried basil
½ teaspoon dried thyme
salt and freshly ground black pepper
100 g/4 oz mushrooms, sliced

1 Heat the oil in a saucepan and fry the onion, green pepper and courgettes gently for 2-3 minutes until they are beginning to soften.
2 Add the lamb, turn the heat to high and fry until the meat is evenly browned, stirring with a wooden spoon to remove any lumps. Pour off any excess fat.
3 Stir in the tomatoes with their juice and the water, breaking up the tomatoes with the spoon. Bring to the boil, stirring frequently.

4 Add the pasta, herbs and salt and pepper to taste and mix well. Cover the pan and simmer the lamb and pasta for 15 minutes.
5 Stir in mushrooms and simmer, uncovered, for 10 minutes. Serve the lamb and pasta medley at once (see Serving ideas and Variations).

Cook's Notes

 TIME
About 45 minutes to prepare and cook.

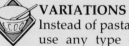 **VARIATIONS**
Instead of pasta shapes, use any type of pasta you may have. Break up spaghetti into small pieces.
Minced beef can be used as an alternative to the lamb.
Dried mixed herbs may be used instead of the dried basil and thyme.

 SERVING IDEAS
This dish needs no accompaniment, but grated hard cheese such as Parmesan or Cheddar may be served separately for sprinkling. Follow with a green salad.

 ECONOMY
Use left-over cooked lamb, chopped finely and added with the tomatoes. Omit all of stage 2.
●570 calories/2375 kj per portion

Farmhouse chicken

SERVES 4

4 chicken pieces, each weighing
    275-400 g/10-14 oz, skinned
salt and freshly ground black pepper
15 g/½ oz margarine or butter
2 tablespoons vegetable oil
100 g/4 oz Italian ribbon noodles
250 g/9 oz carrots, cut into sticks
    about 5 cm/2 inches long and
    5 mm/¼ inch thick
225 g/8 oz frozen sliced green beans,
    defrosted
2 × 300 g/10 oz cans condensed
    mushroom soup
generous pinch of sweet paprika

1 Heat the oven to 180C/350F/Gas 4.
2 Sprinkle the chicken pieces with salt and pepper. Heat the margarine and oil in a large frying-pan and cook the chicken over fairly high heat for 5-10 minutes until browned on all sides. Lower the heat and cook for a further 10-15 minutes, turning the chicken once during this time.
3 Meanwhile, cook the noodles in boiling salted water for 10-12 minutes until *al dente* (tender yet firm to the bite). Cook the carrots in boiling salted water for 5 minutes until tender.
4 Drain the noodles and carrots thoroughly.
5 In a bowl, mix together the noodles, carrots, green beans and mushroom soup. Spoon this mixture into a large shallow ovenproof dish, sprinkle with paprika and place the chicken on top in a single layer.

6 Cover the dish with foil and cook in the oven for 45 minutes or until the chicken is cooked (the juices should run clear when the chicken is pierced with a skewer). Serve hot, straight from the dish.

Cook's Notes

TIME
This dish takes about 30 minutes to prepare (including pre-cooking the chicken, noodles and carrots). Cooking in the oven takes about 45 minutes.

COOK'S TIP
The casserole can be made up to 24 hours in advance, if wished. At the end of stage 5, cover the dish then store in the refrigerator until 1 hour before serving. Cook in the oven as in stage 6 allowing the extra 15 minutes cooking time because the dish will be chilled.

PRESSURE COOKING
Use chicken pieces weighing 225-250 g/8-9 oz. Pre-brown chicken in oil, drain. Add 300 ml/½ pint stock and vegetables. Place trivet on top of chicken and put noodles and 300 ml/½ pint water in a perforated separator lined with foil or in a solid separator. Cover with greaseproof paper and tie down securely. Bring to high (H) pressure and cook for 7 minutes. Release pressure quickly, remove chicken and noodles. Stir in soup, bring to boil and serve on a warmed serving dish.

●495 calories/2075 kj per portion

Chicken lasagne

SERVES 4
6 strips lasagne (see Buying guide)
salt
1 teaspoon vegetable oil
freshly ground black pepper
100 g/4 oz Cheddar cheese, grated
margarine, for greasing

CHICKEN SAUCE
3 tablespoons vegetable oil
1 large onion, sliced
100 g/4 oz streaky bacon, derinded
   and chopped
25 g/1 oz plain flour
300 ml/½ pint chicken stock
225 g/8 oz can tomatoes
250 g/9 oz boneless cooked chicken,
   chopped (see Buying guide)
1 tablespoon tomato purée

WHITE SAUCE
25 g/1 oz margarine or butter
25 g/1 oz plain flour
pinch of freshly grated nutmeg
300 ml/½ pint milk

1 Heat the oven to 180C/350F/Gas 4 and grease a shallow ovenproof dish. ✳
2 Make the chicken sauce: heat the oil in a frying-pan, add the onion and fry gently until soft and lightly coloured. Add the bacon and cook for 1 minute.
3 Sprinkle in the flour and cook for 1 minute, stirring, until straw-coloured. Remove from the heat and gradually stir in stock, tomatoes, chicken and tomato purée.
4 Return to the heat and bring to the boil, stirring constantly, then lower the heat and simmer for 3 minutes. Remove from the heat and set aside.
5 Bring a large pan of salted water to the boil and cook the lasagne with the oil for 10 minutes.
6 Meanwhile, make the white sauce: melt the margarine in a saucepan, sprinkle in the flour and nutmeg and stir over low heat for 2 minutes until straw-coloured. Remove from the heat and gradually stir in the milk, return to the heat again and simmer, stirring, until thick and smooth. Set aside.
7 Drain the lasagne and pat dry with absorbent paper.

8 Spread half the chicken sauce in the bottom of the greased ovenproof dish and sprinkle with salt and pepper. Place 3 strips of lasagne on top.
9 Spread the remaining chicken sauce over the lasagne, sprinkle with more salt and pepper and cover with a second layer of lasagne. Pour the white sauce over the lasagne and sprinkle with salt and pepper.
10 Sprinkle the grated cheese over the top of the white sauce, then bake in the oven for 1 hour until bubbling and golden. If the topping is not golden at the end of the cooking time, heat the grill to high and transfer the lasagne to the grill for 2-3 minutes to brown the cheese. Serve hot, straight from the dish.

Cook's Notes

TIME
Preparation 35 minutes, cooking 1 hour.

BUYING GUIDE
Lasagne varies in width, from one manufacturer to another—'strips' of lasagne are narrow; 'sheets' are wider.
   For 250 g/9 oz boneless chicken, buy 2 large chicken breasts and cook, skin and bone them before using, or buy half a roasted chicken and simply remove the meat.

✳ FREEZING
Do not pre-cook the lasagne strips. Arrange them over the chicken sauce in layers as in stage 8. Cook the made-up dish in a foil freezer container, cool quickly, then seal, label and freeze. Store for up to 1 month. To serve: reheat from frozen, uncovered, in the foil container in a 200C/400F/Gas 6 oven for 1¼ hours until bubbling.

●655 calories/2750 kj per portion

Pork and sweetcorn Stroganoff

SERVES 4
500 g/1 lb pork fillet, cut into 4 cm ×
   5 mm/1½ × ¼ inch strips
freshly ground black pepper
25 g/1 oz margarine or butter
2 tablespoons vegetable oil
1 large onion, finely chopped
250 g/9 oz button mushrooms,
   quartered
200 g/7 oz can sweetcorn, drained
150 ml/¼ pint soured cream
¼ teaspoon freshly grated nutmeg
¼ teaspoon ground cinnamon
salt
sweet paprika, to garnish

1 Heat the oven to 110C/225F/Gas ¼.
2 Season the pork well with pepper.
3 Heat half the margarine and half the oil in a shallow flameproof casserole or large heavy-based frying-pan. Add the onion and fry gently until browned.

4 Add the mushrooms and toss with the onions for 2-3 minutes until just tender. Transfer the onions and mushrooms with their juices to a dish. Keep warm in oven.
5 Wipe the casserole with absorbent paper, then heat the remaining margarine and oil. Add the seasoned pork strips and fry over brisk heat for 2-3 minutes until sealed on all sides (see Cook's tip). Lower the heat and cook for a further 15 minutes, or until cooked through (when cut in half, the pork strips should not be pink inside).
6 Add the reserved onion and mushroom mixture with the sweetcorn and cook over gentle heat for 2 minutes until heated through. Stir in the cream, nutmeg, cinnamon and salt to taste. Heat through gently, but do not boil.
7 Transfer to a warmed serving dish, sprinkle with paprika and serve.

Cook's Notes

TIME
Preparation takes about 15 minutes, cooking about 30 minutes.

SERVING IDEAS
Serve with noodles, preferably fresh, either plain or wholewheat.

COOK'S TIP
If necessary, seal the strips of pork in 2 batches to ensure that they are not crowded in the pan: they must be allowed to seal in the shortest possible time. Keep warm while you seal the remainder.

DID YOU KNOW
This is a variation of the classic Beef Stroganoff— a dish of strips of beef served with soured cream.

●420 calories/1750 kj per portion

chicken catalan

SERVES 6
6 small chicken breasts, skinned
6 tablespoons olive oil
3 medium onions, thinly sliced
2 cloves garlic, crushed
500 g/1 lb long-grain rice
1-2 tablespoons tomato purée
pinch of saffron strands (see
    Steps) or few drops of
    yellow food colouring
1L/2 pints boiling chicken stock
1 teaspoon sweet paprika
salt and freshly ground black pepper
100 g/4 oz Spanish chorizo sausage
    or other firm garlic sausage
    (optional), cut into large chunks
1 green pepper, deseeded and sliced
    into rings
1 red pepper, deseeded and sliced
    into rings
125 g/4 oz stuffed olives
chopped parsley, to garnish

1 Heat half the oil in a large flame - proof casserole. Fry the chicken breasts over moderate heat until golden brown in colour and half cooked through (about 7 minutes each side).

2 Reserve chicken pieces and keep them warm.

3 Add 1 tablespoon more oil to the casserole. Cook the onions over low heat for 2 minutes until transparent but not brown.

4 Add the garlic, the remaining oil and the rice. Stir for a few minutes with a wooden spoon until the rice starts to colour.

5 Meanwhile, stir the tomato purée and colouring, if used, into the boiling stock.

6 Stir stock, with saffron liquid, if used, into the rice mixture, add paprika and salt and pepper to taste, then bring to the boil, stirring constantly.

7 Add the chicken to the casserole with the sausage and peppers, pressing them well down into the rice.

8 Lower the heat, cover and simmer for about 30 minutes or until the rice is just tender, stirring occasionally with a wooden spoon. Be careful not to overcook the rice so that it becomes mushy.

9 Add the olives to the rice and heat through for a few minutes. Taste and adjust seasoning.

10 Transfer to a large warmed serving dish. Sprinkle the chopped parsley over the top to garnish and serve at once.

Cook's Notes

TIME
10-15 minutes for preparation plus 1 hour cooking.

ECONOMY
Chicken breasts are meaty and convenient to use, because they are sold boned or partially boned, but they do tend to be rather expensive. Ordinary chicken pieces are not so expensive as breasts, and they can be used just as well but will need to be cooked for about 10 minutes on each side in stage 1. (You could even buy a whole chicken and joint it yourself.) If you prefer not to have awkward-looking bones in the finished dish, it is quite simple to remove the bones before the chicken is cooked.

DID YOU KNOW
Saffron is an immensely popular spice in Spain, where it is used for colouring rice (it has hardly any taste). It was introduced to the Spaniards by the Arabs, and has for centuries been used as a colouring agent, especially in Arab and Eastern cooking. It is used in this recipe to give the rice a bright, golden-yellow colour, but as it is so expensive, we have suggested yellow food colouring as a cheaper alternative. If you have ground turmeric this can also be used, but it has a more distinctive flavour than saffron. Saffron strands and turmeric are available from delicatessens, good supermarkets and Indian specialist shops.

BUYING GUIDE
Spanish chorizo sausages can be obtained at most good delicatessens, and are easily recognizable by their bright red appearance. They are made from pure pork flavoured with pimiento (hot red pepper), and so are hot and spicy. If you find them difficult to obtain, use any continental-type cured sausage with a spicy flavour.

• 330 calories/1375 kj per portion

54

1 *Crush a few strands of saffron in your fingers and drop them into a small bowl of boiling water.*

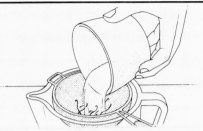

2 *Leave to infuse for at least 2 hours, then strain the water, discarding the saffron strands.*

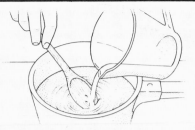

3 *Stir the saffron-coloured liquid into the stock used in recipe.*

Spanish beef casserole

SERVES 4

500 g/1 lb stewing steak, cut into 4 cm/1½ inch cubes
2 tablespoons olive or vegetable oil
1 onion, chopped
1 clove garlic, crushed (optional)
400 g/14 oz can chopped tomatoes
1 red pepper, deseeded and chopped
2 tablespoons medium sherry
8 stuffed green olives, halved
1 thyme sprig or ½ teaspoon dried thyme
salt and freshly ground black pepper

TOPPING
15 g/½ oz butter
1 small onion, finely chopped
175 g/6 oz long-grain rice
300 ml/½ pint boiling water
1 tablespoon grated Parmesan cheese

1 Heat the oven to 180C/350F/Gas 4.
2 Put olive oil in large flameproof casserole, add the onion, garlic, if using, and the stewing steak and fry for 5 minutes.
3 Add the tomatoes, half the red pepper, the sherry, green olives and thyme, and season well with salt and pepper. Bring to the boil, cover, then transfer to the oven and cook for 1¼ hours.
4 Meanwhile, make the topping: melt the butter in a large saucepan, add the onion and fry gently for about 5 minutes until soft.
5 Add the rice and stir until coated with butter. Add the remaining red pepper and season with salt. Add the boiling water, then cover and simmer for about 10-15 minutes, until the rice is tender and all the liquid has evaporated. Remove from heat and stir in cheese.
6 Spread the topping evenly over the meat in the casserole. Return to the oven and cook, uncovered, for a further 20 minutes. Serve at once, straight from the casserole.

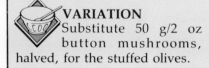

Summer pork curry

SERVES 4

600 g/1¼ lb neck end of pork, trimmed of fat, cut into 2.5 cm/1 inch cubes (see Buying guide)
50 g/2 oz margarine or butter
2 large onions, sliced
2 cloves garlic, crushed (optional)
1 teaspoon ground ginger
1 teaspoon ground turmeric
1 teaspoon chilli powder
2 teaspoons ground cumin
2 teaspoons sweet paprika
1 tablespoon ground coriander
2 tablespoons cornflour
300 ml/½ pint chicken stock
salt and freshly ground black pepper
2 small bananas, thinly sliced
1 large peach, thinly sliced
coriander sprigs, to garnish

CARDAMOM RICE

250 g/9 oz basmati rice or other long grain rice
50 g/2 oz butter
3 cardamom pods, crushed
2 bay leaves
600 ml/1 pint water

1 Melt the margarine in a large flameproof casserole, add onions and the garlic, if using, and fry gently for 5 minutes until soft and lightly coloured. Add the pork and fry over moderate heat, stirring often, until lightly browned on all sides. Stir in the spices and cook for a further 1-2 minutes.

2 In a small bowl, blend the cornflour with a little stock to make a smooth paste. Stir in the remaining stock, then add to the casserole and bring to the boil, stirring constantly, until thick and smooth.

3 Cover and simmer gently for 1¼-1½ hours until pork is tender when pierced with a sharp knife.

4 About 20 minutes before the end of cooking time, make cardamom rice: wash the rice and drain it well. Melt the butter in a large saucepan. Add the rice with the cardamoms and bay leaves and fry gently for 3-4 minutes, stirring well. Pour the water into the pan and bring to the boil. Cover and simmer gently for 10-15 minutes or until rice is tender and the water is absorbed. Discard the cardamoms and bay leaves. Season the rice to taste with pepper and spoon into a warmed serving bowl.

5 Remove the curry from the heat and gently stir in the banana slices, taking care not to break them up. Arrange the peach slices along one side of the casserole. Garnish with coriander sprigs and serve at once, accompanied by the cardamom rice.

Cook's Notes

 TIME
Preparing the curry takes 25-30 minutes, cooking 1¼-1½ hours.

 SERVING IDEAS
Serve with spicy or plain poppadoms, which are available in packets from Indian shops. Hand a bowl of peach or mango chutney separately with the curry.

 BUYING GUIDE
Neck end, one of the less expensive pork cuts, comes from the upper part of the shoulder. It is excellent for casseroled dishes and also for making kebabs.

●910 calories/3825 kj per portion

Paella

The basic essential ingredients for every paella are long-grain rice, olive oil and saffron. After that it can be simple or elaborate, according to the ingredients you use. Vary these to suit your pocket as well as your taste.

You can serve it for a simple summer lunch, or dress it up as a more elaborate, but easy-to-prepare party dish. Paella is perfect for a buffet, as it can so easily be eaten with a fork.

SERVES 6

12 unshelled mussels, defrosted if frozen (see Steps), or 150 g/ 5 oz can or jar mussels, drained
1 kg/2 lb chicken, cut into 8 pieces
100 g/4 oz lean pork fillet, cut into 1 cm/½ inch cubes
salt and freshly ground black pepper
100 ml/3½ fl oz olive oil
2 raw chorizo sausages, cut into 5 mm/¼ inch slices
1 onion, finely chopped
2 cloves garlic, crushed (optional)
1 red pepper, deseeded and cut into 4 cm × 5 mm/1½ × ¼ inch strips
250 g/9 oz tomatoes, skinned, deseeded and finely chopped
1 teaspoon sweet paprika
500 g/1 lb long-grain rice
½ teaspoon saffron strands, crushed and soaked for 2 hours in 1 L/1¾ pints boiling hot chicken stock
250 g/9 oz cooked unpeeled prawns, defrosted if frozen (see Buying guide), or 100 g/4 oz peeled prawns, defrosted if frozen, or 200 g/7 oz can peeled prawns, drained
400 g/14 oz can artichoke hearts, drained
225 g/8 oz frozen peas, defrosted

1 If using unshelled mussels, prepare them as shown in the Steps.
2 Cook the prepared mussels: rinse the soaked mussels thoroughly, then drain. Pour 150 ml/¼ pint water into a heavy frying-pan large enough to hold the mussels in a single layer. Add the mussels, cover and bring to the boil then lower the heat and simmer for 5-6 minutes, shaking the pan gently once or twice. If the mussels have not opened, cook for 1-2 minutes longer. Discard any unopened mussels !and set the rest aside.
3 Season the chicken pieces and pork cubes with salt and pepper. Heat half the oil in a paella pan (see Did you know), large frying-pan, or large, shallow flameproof casserole. Add the chicken and pork and fry over moderate heat for 10-15 minutes, turning frequently, until browned on all sides. After 5 minutes cooking, add the sausage slices to the pan and turn to brown. With a slotted spoon, lift out the meats on to a plate and set aside.
4 Heat the remaining oil in the pan. Add the onion, garlic, if using, pepper strips and chopped tomatoes and cook over gentle heat for about 5 minutes, stirring from time to time, until the onion is soft and the mixture well blended. Stir in the paprika. Cook for 1 minute. Remove from heat. Stir in rice.
5 Strain the saffron stock into the pan and stir once. Bring to the boil and cook for 5 minutes.
6 Arrange the chicken, pork, sausages, cooked mussels, prawns and artichoke hearts on top of the rice. Sprinkle over the peas.
7 Turn down heat to low. Cook for 12-15 minutes, until rice is tender and all liquid absorbed.
8 Turn off the heat under the pan. Cover the pan with a lid or drape it with a kitchen towel. Leave for 3-4 minutes, to allow the flavours to blend. Serve straight from the pan.

TO CLEAN MUSSELS

1 *Check mussels are really fresh: tap any open ones against work surface. Discard if they do not shut.*

2 *Pull away any beards (pieces of hanging seaweed gripped between the 2 shells of the mussel).*

3 *Scrub mussels under cold running water, then scrape away encrustations with a sharp knife. Then soak mussels in fresh cold water to cover for 2-3 hours. Change the water several times.*

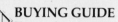

TIME
Preparation takes about 1¼ hours if using un-shelled mussels. Allow a further 2-3 hours for soaking the mussels and saffron threads. Cooking the paella takes about 45 minutes.

WATCHPOINT
It is absolutely vital to discard any unopened mussels—this shows they are not fresh, which can cause serious food poisoning.

BUYING GUIDE
Try to buy mussels and prawns in the shell, as they look so attractive in the finished dish. Both are available from high-quality fishmongers, and frozen from freezer centres and some supermarkets.

SERVING IDEAS
Serve the paella at the table straight from the pan, as the Spaniards do.

The paella is usually eaten by itself—a vegetable accompaniment is not necessary.

VARIATIONS
In Spain, paella is often made with rabbit, and this could be substituted for chicken.

For a special occasion, add some lobster meat to the paella.

DID YOU KNOW
The name paella comes from *paellera*, the pan in which the dish is traditionally cooked in Spain: it is shallow with gently sloping sides and 2 flattened handles. You can buy special paella pans from high-quality kitchen equipment shops or departments of big stores—or, better still, buy one on holiday in Spain. But if you do not have a *paellera*, a large heavy frying-pan, preferably with a lid, or a large, shallow flameproof casserole will do very well instead for making the paella.

●980 calories/4100 kj per portion

Spicy roast chicken

SERVES 4-6
1.5 kg/3-3½ lb oven-ready chicken
25 g/1 oz butter, softened
1 teaspoon ground turmeric
1 teaspoon ground ginger
¼ teaspoon cayenne
vegetable oil, for greasing

STUFFING
2 tablespoons vegetable oil
1 onion, finely chopped
1 large red pepper, deseeded and
**   finely chopped**
2 garlic cloves, crushed (optional)
100 g/4 oz long-grain rice
350 ml/12 fl oz hot chicken stock
4 tablespoons flaked almonds
finely grated zest of 1 lime
1 tablespoon fresh lime juice
½ teaspoon ground turmeric
½ teaspoon ground ginger
¼ teaspoon cayenne
salt and freshly ground black pepper

1 Make the stuffing: heat the oil in a saucepan, add the onion, red pepper and garlic, if using, and fry gently for 5 minutes until the onion is soft and lightly coloured. Add the rice and fry for 1-2 minutes, stirring constantly, then pour in the hot stock. Bring to the boil, stir once, then lower the heat, cover and simmer very gently for about 20 minutes until the rice is cooked and all the liquid has been absorbed.
2 Transfer the rice and vegetables to a bowl, stir in the remaining stuffing ingredients with salt and pepper to taste and leave to cool.
3 Heat the oven to 190C/375F/Gas 5 and grease a small ovenproof dish.
4 Wipe the chicken inside and out with absorbent paper. Spoon about one-third of the stuffing mixture into the neck end of the chicken. Fold the neck skin back into position, then fold the wing tips over it. Secure with a metal skewer. Spoon the remaining stuffing into the prepared dish. Cover with foil.
5 Place the chicken in a roasting tin.

Prick the skin all over, except for the stuffed area. Mix the butter, spices, together with salt and pepper to taste, and brush over chicken.
6 Roast the prepared chicken in the oven for about 1½ hours, until tender (the juices run clear when the thigh is pierced with a skewer). Baste the chicken occasionally during the cooking time. Halfway through cooking time, place the dish of stuffing on the shelf below the chicken to cook.
7 Transfer the chicken to a warmed serving dish, remove the skewer and keep the chicken warm in the oven turned to its lowest setting. Skim the fat from the juices in the roasting tin and pour juices over chicken. Serve carved into slices, with stuffing (see Serving ideas).

Cook's Notes

TIME
Preparing the stuffing takes about 25 minutes. Allow 30 minutes for cooling. Preparation then takes 10 minutes, cooking 1½ hours.

COOK'S TIP
The stuffing can be made ahead of time, but to avoid any risk of salmonella it should not be used to stuff the

chicken until just before roasting. There should always be a free circulation of air in the centre of the bird.

SERVING IDEAS
Serve with a stir-fried mixture of vegetables such as cauliflower florets, beansprouts and carrot strips.

●645 calories/2700 kj per portion

60

Lamb chops in tomato rice

SERVES 4

4 thick lamb chump chops, trimmed
  of excess fat
15 g/½ oz margarine or butter
2 tablespoons vegetable oil
1 onion, chopped
1 celery stalk, chopped
400 g/14 oz can tomatoes, chopped
300 ml/½ pint water
200 g/7 oz long-grain rice
1 tablespoon chopped fresh basil or
  1 teaspoon dried basil
salt and freshly ground black pepper
basil sprigs, to garnish (optional)

1 Heat the margarine with the oil in a large frying-pan with a lid. Add the chops and fry over brisk heat for 5-10 minutes, turning once, to brown on both sides. Remove from the pan and set aside.

2 Add the onion and celery to the pan and fry gently for 5 minutes until soft and lightly coloured. Stir in the tomatoes with their juice, add the water and bring the mixture to the boil.

3 Add the rice, basil and salt and pepper to taste and stir well. Return the chops to the pan and cover them with the tomato and rice mixture.

4 Cover the pan and simmer gently for 30-40 minutes or until the chops are cooked through (the juices should run clear when they are pierced with a sharp knife), the rice is tender and all the liquid has been absorbed.

5 Taste and adjust seasoning. Transfer to a warm serving dish and garnish with basil sprigs, if liked. Serve at once.

Cook's Notes

TIME
Preparation takes about 10 minutes, cooking 45-55 minutes.

COOK'S TIP
This dish needs no vegetable accompaniment, but serve a green salad to follow.

VARIATIONS
The flavour of basil goes especially well with tomatoes, but if unavailable, thyme would also be good.

Pork chops may be used instead of lamb, in which case sage could be used instead of basil.

●780 calories/3250 kj per portion

Apricot-stuffed lamb

SERVES 8
1.8 kg/4 lb shoulder of lamb, boned with pocket for stuffing, and bones reserved (see Buying guide)
1 teaspoon ground coriander

TO GARNISH
apricot halves
mint sprigs

STUFFING
2 tablespoons vegetable oil
1 onion, finely chopped
50 g/2 oz long-grain rice, cooked
100 g/4 oz dried apricots, soaked overnight, drained and chopped
finely grated zest of 1 large orange
1 tablespoon ground coriander
salt and freshly ground black pepper

1 Heat the oven to 200C/400F/Gas 6.
2 Make the stuffing: heat the oil in a saucepan, add the onion and fry gently for 5 minutes until soft and lightly coloured. Remove from the heat, add the rice, apricots, orange zest, coriander and salt and pepper to taste and stir all the ingredients to mix very thoroughly.
3 Open out the lamb and lay it skin side down on a board or work surface. Sprinkle with the coriander and season with salt and pepper, then spoon the stuffing into the boned cavity, packing it in well. Fold the 2 long sides of the lamb over the stuffing to overlap and form into a neat roll (see Preparation). Tie the stuffed rolled lamb at intervals with fine string.
4 Place the lamb bones in a roasting tin. Set a rack over the bones and place the lamb on the rack. Roast in the oven for 30 minutes, then lower the heat to 180C/350F/Gas 4 and roast for a further 1½ hours until the lamb is tender and cooked through (the juices run clear when the meat is pierced with a fine skewer).
5 Remove the string and transfer the lamb to a warmed serving dish. Leave in a warm place for 10 minutes to allow the meat to 'settle', to make it easier to carve.
6 Carve the lamb into slices, garnish with apricot halves and mint sprigs. Serve the lamb at once, with a gravy made from the pan juices handed separately in a warmed sauceboat, if liked.

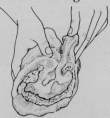

Moroccan stuffed lamb

SERVES 4-6
2 kg/4 lb boned shoulder of lamb, trimmed and tied
25 g/1 oz margarine or butter
1 small onion, chopped
1 clove garlic, crushed (optional)
1 celery stalk, chopped
200 ml/7 fl oz water
50 g/2 oz long-grain rice
¼ teaspoon ground cardamom
2 tablespoons chopped fresh mint or 1 tablespoon dried mint
salt and freshly ground black pepper
25 g/1 oz flaked almonds, toasted
2-3 tablespoons seedless raisins
1 egg, beaten

1 Heat the oven to 230C/450F/Gas 8.
2 Melt the margarine in a small frying-pan. Add the onion, garlic, if using, and celery and fry for 5 minutes over gentle heat until soft and lightly coloured. With a slotted spoon, transfer to a bowl.
3 Bring the water to the boil in a saucepan. Add the rice, cardamom, half the mint and salt to taste and stir well. Cover the pan and simmer very gently for 15-20 minutes or until the rice is tender and all the water has been absorbed.
4 Mix the rice with the vegetables in the bowl and stir in the almonds, raisins and the remaining mint. Season to taste with salt and pepper and stir well. Mix in the egg to bind, forking it through ingredients.
5 Spoon the stuffing into the cavity in the lamb. Roll up snugly and tie at intervals with fine string.
6 Place the lamb, fat side up, on a rack in a roasting tin. Roast in the oven for 20 minutes, then turn down the heat to 180C/350F/Gas 4. Continue roasting for 1-1½ hours or until the lamb is cooked to your liking (for medium-done meat the juices run slightly pink when the meat is pierced with a sharp knife, for well-done they run clear).

Cook's Notes

TIME
Preparation, including making the stuffing mixture, takes about 40 minutes. Cooking in the oven takes 1½-2 hours.

SERVING IDEAS
There is no need to serve potatoes or any other form of carbohydrate with this lamb because of the rice in the stuffing. Instead, serve vegetables such as carrots or garden peas. Mint sprigs, if available, make an attractive garnish.

●805 calories/3375 kj per portion

7 Remove the string and leave the lamb to 'rest' for 10 minutes before carving (this makes carving easier). Transfer the lamb to a warmed serving platter to carve.

SNACKS AND SAUCES

Tortellini with tomato sauce

SERVES 4
500 g/1 lb tortellini (see Buying guide)
salt
4 slices processed cheese (see For children)

SAUCE
400 g/14 oz can tomatoes
1 onion, chopped
few sprigs parsley
salt
25 g/1 oz margarine
25 g/1 oz plain flour
1 teaspoon tomato purée
1 teaspoon clear honey
freshly ground black pepper

1 Make sauce: work the tomatoes, onion and the parsley sprigs in a blender and add ½ teaspoon salt.
2 Melt the margarine in a saucepan,

sprinkle in the flour and stir over low heat for 1-2 minutes until straw-coloured. Gradually stir in the puréed mixture, then add tomato purée and honey. Season to taste with salt and pepper. Simmer very gently for 20 minutes, until the sauce is thick and quite smooth.
3 Meanwhile, bring a large pan of salted water to the boil and cook the

tortellini for 3-4 minutes if fresh (or according to packet instructions, if dried). Meanwhile, heat the grill to high. Drain pasta thoroughly and divide between 4 individual flame-proof dishes. Pour over the tomato sauce and place a cheese slice on top. Place the dishes under the grill for about 3 minutes, until cheese is melted. Serve at once.

Cook's Notes

 TIME
Preparing and cooking take only 45 minutes.

 BUYING GUIDE
Tortellini makes a very useful standby for a quick snack or supper dish. Fresh tortellini are sold loose or packed in plastic boxes from delicatessens and some large supermarkets. They can be either plain or green and stuffed with either a meat or cheese

filling. Dried varieties are sold in packets at most supermarkets. All are suitable for this dish.

FOR CHILDREN
Use animal-shaped or other fancy biscuit cutters to cut cheese slices into fun shapes. But watch the grill-ing – if the cheese melts too much the cheese figures will lose their distinctive shapes.

●380 calories/1575 kj per portion

Crispy stuffed cannelloni

SERVES 4
8 cannelloni tubes (see Buying
   guide)
salt
3 tablespoons vegetable oil
1 onion, finely chopped
175 g/6 oz curd cheese
75 g/3 oz ham, finely chopped
50 g/2 oz shelled walnuts, finely
   chopped
2 teaspoons tomato purée
8 black olives, stoned and chopped
2 tablespoons chopped fresh
   parsley
freshly ground black pepper
1 egg
3 tablespoons fresh breadcrumbs
2 tablespoons grated Parmesan
   cheese
vegetable oil, for deep-frying

1 Bring a large pan of salted water to
the boil. Add 1 tablespoon of the oil
and then the cannelloni. Bring back
to the boil and simmer for 4-5
minutes. Drain, rinse under cold
water, pat dry and leave to cool.
2 Heat the remaining oil in a frying-
pan, add the onion and fry gently for
10 minutes until soft and browned.
Remove from the pan with a slotted
spoon and drain on absorbent paper
for a few minutes.
3 Cream the curd cheese in a bowl
with a wooden spoon. Beat in the
fried onion, chopped ham, walnuts,
tomato purée, olives and parsley.
Season to taste with salt and pepper
and mix well.
4 Using a teaspoon, push spoonfuls
of the mixture into the cannelloni
tubes, filling them evenly (see
Preparation).
5 Beat the egg in a shallow dish. Mix
the breadcrumbs and Parmesan
cheese together on a large flat plate.
Dip the cannelloni tubes into the
egg, then roll them in the breadcrumbs and cheese until evenly
coated with the mixture.
6 Pour enough oil into a deep-fat
frier to cover the cannelloni tubes.
Heat to 190C/375F or until a stale
bread cube browns in 50 seconds.
7 Using a slotted spoon, lower 4
cannelloni at a time into the hot oil
and deep-fry for 2-3 minutes until
golden brown on all sides. Drain on
absorbent paper and keep warm
while frying remainder. Serve hot.

Cook's Notes

 **TIME**
The stuffed cannelloni
tubes take about 20
minutes to pre-cook and
prepare. Frying time is 4-6
minutes.

PREPARATION
To fill the cannelloni
tubes for frying:

*Use a teaspoon to fill the can-
nelloni tubes—gently push in the
mixture.*

 BUYING GUIDE
Be sure to buy the
cannelloni that are for
boiling not those used for baked
dishes.

 SERVING IDEAS
Serve with a green salad
or, to make a more
substantial supper dish, with
French fried potatoes as well.

 VARIATIONS
Use full-fat soft cheese
instead of curd cheese if
curd is not available.

●430 calories/1800 kj per portion

Pasta kugel

SERVES 4
200 g/7 oz wholewheat pasta rings
3 eggs
225 g/8 oz curd cheese
150 ml/¼ pint soured cream
2 tablespoons soft brown sugar
100 g/4 oz seedless raisins
¼ teaspoon salt
¼ teaspoon ground cinnamon
¼ teaspoon freshly grated nutmeg
margarine, for greasing

TOPPING
2 tablespoons chopped mixed nuts
¼ teaspoon ground cinnamon
15 g/½ oz butter

1 Heat the oven to 180C/350F/Gas 4. Grease a 1 L/2 pint ovenproof dish generously with margarine.
2 Bring a pan of salted water to the boil and cook the pasta rings for

12 minutes or according to packet instructions until they are cooked but still firm to the bite.
3 Meanwhile, beat the eggs in a bowl, add the curd cheese, soured cream and sugar and beat with a fork until smooth. Mix in the raisins, salt and spices.
4 Drain the cooked pasta rings and return them to the rinsed-out pan. Pour the curd cheese mixture over

the pasta and stir it until evenly coated. Transfer the mixture to the prepared dish, sprinkle with nuts and cinnamon and dot the surface with the butter.
5 Bake in the oven, uncovered, for about 30 minutes, until the top is golden and filling has set around the edge but is still creamy in the middle. Serve at once straight from the dish (see Serving ideas).

Cook's Notes

 TIME
20 minutes preparation and about 30 minutes baking in the oven.

 DID YOU KNOW
Kugel is the Jewish name for a pudding, usually made of noodles or potatoes and baked. Although many kugels, like this one, are semi-sweet, they are not meant to be served as desserts.

SERVING IDEAS
This wholewheat pasta kugel makes a tasty brunch, lunch or supper dish, served with green salad or fruit, such as sliced pears or peaches.

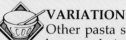 **VARIATION**
Other pasta shapes can be used instead of rings, such as shells or wheels.

●535 calories/2250 kj per portion

Spaghetti with meat balls

SERVES 4

350 g/12 oz spaghetti
3 tablespoons vegetable oil
1 onion, chopped
1 clove garlic, crushed (optional)
400 g/14 oz can tomatoes
75 ml/3 fl oz hot chicken stock
1 tablespoon tomato purée
¼ teaspoon dried thyme
1 teaspoon dried oregano
salt and freshly ground black pepper
500 g/1 lb minced beef
2 tablespoons chopped fresh
  parsley
a knob of butter, for tossing
grated Parmesan cheese (optional)

1 Heat 1 tablespoon oil in a large saucepan, add the onion and garlic, if using, and fry gently for 5 minutes until soft and lightly coloured. Add the tomatoes with their liquid, the stock, tomato purée, thyme and half the oregano. Season to taste with salt and pepper. Bring to the boil, cover and simmer for 30-40 minutes.
2 Meanwhile, in a bowl mix the beef with the remaining oregano and the parsley and season well with salt and pepper. Shape into 32 small balls.
3 Heat the rest of the oil in a frying-pan over moderate heat and fry the meat balls on all sides for 6-8 minutes until golden brown. Drain on absorbent paper and keep warm.
4 Bring a pan of salted water to the boil and cook the spaghetti for about 10 minutes until *al dente* (tender, yet firm to the bite).
5 Meanwhile, sieve the tomato sauce, or purée in a blender. Return to the pan to reheat, adding a little water if the sauce is too thick. Stir in the meat balls and then transfer to a warmed serving dish.
6 Drain the pasta thoroughly and toss in butter. Transfer to warmed individual serving bowls. Spoon 8 meat balls and a quarter of the sauce over each spaghetti serving. Serve at once, with cheese, if liked.

Cook's Notes

TIME
This dish takes about 1 hour to prepare and cook.

SERVING IDEAS
This dish makes a quite filling lunch on its own. For dinner, serve with some crusty white bread and a crisp green salad.

VARIATION
Instead of the stock use the same quantity of red wine and perhaps drink the rest with the meal!

●685 calories/2875 kj per portion

Spaghetti alla bolognese

SERVES 4

500 g/1 lb spaghetti
2 tablespoons vegetable oil
1 bacon rasher, derinded and finely chopped
¼ onion, finely chopped
5-cm/2-inch piece of carrot, finely chopped
5-cm/2-inch piece of celery, finely chopped
1 clove garlic, finely chopped (optional)
175 g/6 oz finely minced lean beef (see Buying guide)
4 tablespoons Italian dry red wine or beef stock
175 g/6 oz Italian plum tomatoes, chopped, or 225 g/8 oz can tomatoes, chopped
pinch of freshly grated nutmeg
¼ - ½ teaspoon dried oregano
salt and freshly ground black pepper
50 g/2 oz grated Parmesan cheese, to serve

1 Heat the oil in a large frying-pan, add the bacon, onion, carrot, celery and garlic, if using, and fry over moderate heat for about 10 minutes until the vegetables are softened, stirring occasionally.
2 Add the beef, turn the heat to high and fry until the meat is evenly browned on all sides, stirring with a wooden spoon to remove any lumps.
3 Stir in the wine and bring to the boil, then lower the heat again and simmer for about 10-15 minutes until the wine has reduced.
4 Stir in the tomatoes with their juice and bring to the boil. Lower the heat, add the nutmeg, oregano and salt and pepper to taste, and cook for about 30 minutes, stirring occasionally. Add more water if the sauce becomes too dry.
5 Meanwhile, cook the spaghetti in a large saucepan of boiling salted water for 10-12 minutes or until *al dente* (tender, yet firm to the bite).
6 Drain thoroughly, transfer to a warmed serving dish, then pour over the sauce. Serve at once, sprinkled with grated Parmesan cheese.

Cook's Notes

 TIME
About 10 minutes to prepare and about 1 hour to cook.

 FREEZING
The bolognese sauce freezes extremely well: transfer to a rigid container, leaving headspace, cool quickly then seal, label and freeze for up to 3 months. To serve: put frozen sauce in a heavy-based saucepan with 1-2 tablespoons water and heat gently until bubbling, stirring frequently.

 BUYING GUIDE
The secret of making a good bolognese sauce which is smooth in texture, lies in the quality of the beef you buy. Buy a piece of chuck steak and mince it at home, or ask the butcher to do it for you.

●705 calories/2950 kj per portion

Frankfurter and macaroni supper

SERVES 4

6 frankfurters, cut into 2.5 cm/1 inch
   lengths
salt
175 g/6 oz short-cut macaroni
2 tablespoons vegetable oil
2 onions, sliced
1 green pepper, deseeded and
   chopped
2 tomatoes, skinned, deseeded and
   chopped
1 tablespoon cornflour
150 g/5 oz natural yoghurt
1 tablespoon tomato purée
¼ teaspoon dried mixed herbs
freshly ground black pepper
2-3 tablespoons milk (optional)

TO GARNISH
2 tomatoes, skinned and sliced
parsley sprigs

1 Heat the oven to 220C/425F/Gas 7.
2 Bring a pan of salted water to the
boil, add the macaroni and cook for
about 15 minutes until just tender.
3 Meanwhile, heat the oil in a large
frying-pan, add the onions, green
pepper and frankfurters and fry over
moderate heat for 5 minutes, or until
the onions are soft and lightly
coloured. Stir in the tomatoes and
cook, stirring occasionally, for a
further 5 minutes.
4 Put the cornflour into a bowl and
blend to a smooth paste with 1-2
tablespoons of yoghurt. Gradually
stir in the remaining yoghurt, then
the tomato purée, herbs and salt and
pepper to taste.
5 Pour the mixture over the vegetables in the frying-pan and bring to
the boil, stirring constantly.
Remove from the heat.
6 Drain the macaroni, rinse under
hot running water, then drain again
thoroughly and add to the vegetable
mixture. Fold the macaroni into the
vegetable mixture, adding a little
milk if the sauce seems too thick. ✳
7 Transfer the mixture to a 1.5 L/2½
pint ovenproof casserole and bake
in the oven, uncovered, for 10-15
minutes (see Cook's tip).
8 Garnish with the tomato slices
and a few parsley sprigs, then serve
hot, straight from the casserole.

Cook's Notes

TIME
This dish takes a total of
45 minutes to prepare
and cook.

FREEZING
At the end of stage 6,
transfer to a rigid con-
tainer, cool quickly, cover then
seal, label and freeze for up to 3
months. To serve: defrost at
room temperature for 4 hours,
then turn into a casserole and
continue from the beginning of
stage 7, allowing an extra 10
minutes or so baking time.

COOK'S TIP
The dish can be finished
off under a pre-heated
moderate grill, rather than in
the oven, as long as the mixture
is kept hot during each stage of
preparation.

DID YOU KNOW
In America this dish is
often called Frank and
Mac from the shortened names
of the two main ingredients in
the dish.

●435 calories/1825 kj per portion

Deep-fried ravioli

MAKES 30
225 g/8 oz plain flour
large pinch salt
50 g/2 oz butter, diced
2 eggs, separated
75 ml/3 fl oz water
vegetable oil, for deep frying
basil leaves, to garnish

FILLING
75 g/3 oz Gruyère cheese, finely diced
75 g/3 oz cooked ham, finely chopped
1 tablespoon finely chopped fresh parsley
1 tablespoon chopped fresh basil
1 egg
salt and freshly ground black pepper

1 Make the filling: mix together the cheese, ham and herbs in a medium-sized bowl. In another bowl beat the egg with a little salt and freshly ground black pepper. Cover both and refrigerate.

2 Sift the flour and salt into a large bowl. Add the butter and rub it in with the fingertips until the mixture resembles fine breadcrumbs. Make a well in the centre, add egg yolks and water and mix to a soft dough.
3 Turn out on to a lightly floured surface and knead gently until dough is no longer sticky. Roll out to a rectangle about 38 × 25 cm/ 15 × 10 inches and cut out about thirty 6.5 cm/2½ inch circles.
4 Lightly beat the egg whites. Brush the edges of the circles with the egg whites and place a teaspoon of the filling in the centre of each one. Fold each over the edges, to form semi-circles. Press the edges together to seal.
5 Meanwhile, pour enough oil into a deep-fat frier with a basket to come halfway up the sides. Heat the oil to 190C/375F or until a stale bread cube turns golden in 50 seconds. Fry ravioli, in batches of 10, until golden brown.
6 Remove and drain on absorbent paper. Fry the remaining ravioli, reheating the oil between batches. Pile the cooked ravioli on to a serving plate and serve at once, garnished with basil leaves.

Mustard chicken livers

SERVES 4
350 g/12 oz chicken livers, cut into
   2.5 cm/1 inch pieces (see
   Preparation and Cook's tip)
25 g/1 oz butter
1 large onion, roughly chopped
2 tablespoons grainy mustard
¼ teaspoon made English mustard
4 tablespoons single cream
salt and freshly ground black pepper
3 spring onions, sliced

SAVOURY NOODLES
175 g/6 oz tagliatelle
1 tablespoon corn oil
25 g/1 oz shelled walnuts, roughly
   chopped
2 tomatoes, diced

1 Melt the butter in a saucepan, add the onion and fry gently for 5 minutes until soft and lightly coloured. Add chicken livers and continue cooking for 10 minutes, stirring frequently.

Cook's Notes

 TIME
15 minutes preparation;
20 minutes cooking.

 COOK'S TIP
Frozen chicken livers may be used, but they must be defrosted and drained thoroughly first.

 VARIATIONS
Lamb kidneys are also suitable for this recipe: cut in half and remove the centre cores. Allow 2 or 3 more minutes cooking time at stage 3.
   Instead of tagliatelle, use pasta shapes or long-grain rice.

 PREPARATION
Gall bladders must be removed from the livers:

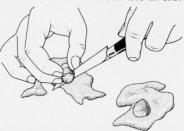

If pierced, their bitter fluid taints the flesh. Cut out with a small section of liver around and trim any green-tinged flesh.

●445 calories/1875 kj per portion

2 Meanwhile, bring a pan of salted water to the boil and cook the tagliatelle for 8-10 minutes until soft but still firm to the bite.
3 Add the mustards and cream to the chicken livers and season to taste with salt and black pepper. Continue cooking very gently for a further 5 minutes.

4 Drain the tagliatelle thoroughly and put it into a bowl. Immediately add the oil, walnuts and tomatoes and mix together thoroughly.
5 Spoon the tagliatelle mixture on to warmed serving plates. Sprinkle over the spring onions, then spoon the chicken liver mixture on top. Serve at once, while still hot.

Tangy fish fingers

SERVES 4
12 fish fingers
2 tablespoons cornflour
150 ml/¼ pint chicken stock
225 g/8 oz can pineapple pieces
    (see Buying guide)
2 tablespoons soy sauce
pinch of ground ginger
2 teaspoons tomato purée
25 g/1 oz soft brown sugar
1 tablespoon vinegar
salt and freshly ground black pepper
½ red pepper, deseeded and diced
4 spring onions, chopped
1 tablespoon vegetable oil
225 g/8 oz long-grain rice
600 ml/1 pint boiling water
1 teaspoon dried mixed herbs

1 In a bowl, blend the cornflour with a little stock to make a smooth paste, then gradually stir in the remaining stock.

2 Put the pineapple pieces, with their juice, into a saucepan with the soy sauce, ginger, tomato purée, sugar and vinegar. Pour in the thickened chicken stock and season to taste with salt and pepper.

3 Add the red pepper and spring onions to the pan and bring to the boil, stirring. Lower the heat, cover the pan and leave to simmer, stirring occasionally while cooking the rice.

4 Heat the grill to moderate. Heat the oil in a large saucepan over low heat, add the rice and stir to coat the grains thoroughly. Pour in the boiling water (see Cook's tips) add the herbs and stir once. Bring to the boil, then simmer, covered, for about 15 minutes, until the rice is

tender and the cooking liquid is all absorbed. [!]

5 While the rice is cooking, grill the fish fingers for 8-10 minutes, turning once, until golden on both sides. Cut each fish finger into 3-4 bite-sized pieces.

6 Divide the rice between 4 warmed plates.

7 Place the fish finger pieces on top of the rice, dividing them equally between the portions. Spoon the hot sauce over each portion and serve at once.

Cook's Notes

 TIME
Preparation and cooking take about 35 minutes, including the rice.

 FOR CHILDREN
Children will enjoy this dish, although the red pepper is perhaps best omitted if serving to very young children and toddlers.

 VARIATIONS
Instead of using fish fingers, stir 150 g/5 oz roughly chopped cooked pork into the sauce before serving with the rice.

 BUYING GUIDE
Canned pineapple pieces are less expensive than chunks or rings. If they are not available, buy pineapple chunks, chop them and use in the same way.

[!] WATCHPOINT
Remove the pan from the heat as soon as the rice is cooked, so that it does not catch.

 COOK'S TIPS
Coating the rice grains with oil ensures that they stay separate during cooking.
    Simmering the rice in twice its volume of boiling water, which is absorbed by the end of cooking, gives a really fluffy result.

● 490 calories/2050 kj per portion

Kabanos fiesta

SERVES 4

2 tablespoons vegetable oil
1 onion, finely chopped
1 small green pepper, deseeded
and finely chopped
400 g/14 oz can tomatoes
1 teaspoon sweet paprika
½ teaspoon sugar
salt and freshly ground black pepper
175 g/6 oz kabanos sausages, cut
into 1 cm/½ inch slices (see
Buying guide)
350 g/12 oz cooked long-grain rice
(see Cook's tip)
2 tablespoons chopped parsley, to
garnish

1 Heat the oil in a saucepan and fry the onion and the pepper over moderate heat for 3 minutes until soft and lightly browned.

2 Add the tomatoes and their juice, paprika, sugar, and salt and pepper to taste. Bring to the boil, breaking up the tomatoes with a wooden spoon and simmer, uncovered, for about 10 minutes, stirring the tomato sauce from time to time.

3 Add the kabanos and rice to the sauce, stir well and simmer for a further 5 minutes or until piping hot all the way through.

4 Serve immediately in a warmed serving dish, garnished with the chopped parsley.

Sauces
for a pasta party

With fresh pasta now so widely available at delicatessens and supermarkets, an easy way to entertain friends is to hold a pasta party. The sauces given below combine perfectly with any type of fresh pasta. All you need to serve with them is a green salad tossed in a well-flavoured dressing and some Italian wine. Prepare the sauces in advance and then cook the pasta once your friends have arrived.

For this menu, buy plain white pasta made with egg, or green or wholewheat pasta. Choose tagliatelle or spaghetti, and allow about 100 g/4 oz per person. Alternatively, make your own pasta with a pasta machine (available from specialist kitchen shops and large department stores) — just follow manufacturer's instructions.

To cook 500 g/1 lb fresh pasta, add about 1 tablespoon salt to a large saucepan of water, then bring to the boil. Add the pasta, bring back to the boil, then lower the heat slightly, stir once and simmer for about 3 minutes until *al dente* (tender, yet firm to the bite). Drain in a colander and serve at once with the sauce separately.

Creamy Gorgonzola sauce

SERVES 4-6
100 g/4 oz Gorgonzola cheese, cut into small pieces (see Buying guide)
150 ml/¼ pint milk
50 g/2 oz butter
50 ml/2 fl oz double cream
freshly ground black pepper
finely chopped parsley, to garnish

COUNTDOWN
The day before
●Make the Creamy Gorgonzola sauce up to the end of stage 1, then cover closely with cling film and refrigerate.
●Make the Pesto up to the end of stage 2, then cover and refrigerate.
●Make the Ham provençal sauce, then cover and refrigerate.

1 Pour the milk into a heavy-based saucepan and heat gently until hot but not simmering. Add the cheese and butter and stir gently with a wooden spoon until smooth.
2 Add the cream to the pan with pepper to taste and heat through gently. Do not allow the sauce to simmer. Serve at once, straight from the pan.

Pesto

SERVES 4-6
50 g/2 oz fresh basil leaves
bunch of fresh parsley
40 g/1½ oz pine nuts
2 cloves garlic
225 ml/8 fl oz olive oil
75 g/3 oz Parmesan cheese, freshly grated
50 g/2 oz butter, softened and cut into small pieces
¼ teaspoon sugar
¼ teaspoon salt
freshly ground black pepper
1 tablespoon pasta cooking water

1 Put the basil, parsley, pine nuts and garlic in a blender or food processor and work until finely chopped.
2 With machine running, slowly pour in the olive oil, then add the Parmesan cheese followed by the butter, sugar and salt. Season to

2 hours before
●Make the salad.
5 minutes before
●Cook the pasta.
●Add the cream to the Gorgonzola sauce and heat through.
●Reheat the Ham provençal sauce.
Just before serving
●Stir 1 tablespoon of the pasta water into the Pesto.

taste with pepper, then transfer to a pan or bowl (see Storage).
3 Just before serving, add the tablespoon of pasta cooking water, stir well and serve at once.

Ham provençal sauce

SERVES 4-6
1 tablespoon olive oil
15 g/½ oz butter
100 g/4 oz pancetta bacon, finely diced (see Buying guide)
1 onion, sliced
1 clove garlic, thinly sliced (optional)
600 g/1 lb 5 oz canned tomatoes
1 tablespoon tomato purée
1 teaspoon Italian herb seasoning or dried mixed herbs
½ teaspoon freshly ground black pepper
salt

1 Heat the oil and butter in a large frying-pan. Add the bacon and fry for 2 minutes. Add the onion and garlic, if using, and fry for a further 3 minutes until soft.
2 Stir in the tomatoes, tomato purée, herb seasoning and pepper. Bring to the boil, then lower the heat, cover the pan and simmer for 20 minutes. Season to taste with salt and serve the sauce at once, straight from the pan.

Cook's Notes

Creamy Gorgonzola sauce

TIME
This sauce takes just 10 minutes to make.

BUYING GUIDE
Gorgonzola is an Italian blue-veined cheese, with a strong flavour and a creamy texture which melts easily. Italian Dolcelatte cheese can be used with the same results, but the flavour will be considerably milder.

●270 calories/1125 kj per portion

Pesto

TIME
This sauce takes about 5 minutes to make in a blender or food processor.

STORAGE
Covered tightly, pesto can be kept in the refrigerator for about 1 week.

DID YOU KNOW
Pesto is the famous basil sauce from the port of Genoa in northern Italy, where basil grows prolifically. It is used there mostly as a sauce for all kinds of pasta and as a flavouring for soups.

For an authentic flavour, it is most important to use fresh basil and grated fresh Parmesan cheese – the latter is available from most delicatessens and some large supermarkets.

●680 calories/2850 kj per portion

Ham provençal sauce

TIME
10 minutes preparation, 20 minutes cooking.

BUYING GUIDE
Pancetta is an Italian raw, fatty bacon with a distinctive, sweetish flavour. It is available from most good delicatessens and Italian food shops. As an alternative, use smoked streaky bacon.

SERVING IDEAS
Serve with topping of grated Parmesan.

●160 calories/675 kj per portion

Vegetables in curry sauce

SERVES 4

1 small cauliflower, divided into
    florets
250 g/9 oz small carrots, scraped and
    thickly sliced
250 g/9 oz French beans, trimmed
    and cut into chunks
250 g/9 oz shelled broad beans
salt

SAUCE
25 g/1 oz butter
25 g/1 oz plain flour
1 tablespoon mild curry powder
large pinch of ground ginger
300 ml/½ pint milk
2 tablespoons fresh orange juice
freshly ground black pepper
2 tablespoons single cream or
    top of the milk
1 tablespoon blanched almonds,
    halved
1 tablespoon chopped mint or
    parsley

1 Cook all the prepared vegetables together in boiling salted water until they are just tender — no more than 10 minutes. Do not allow them to become soft. Drain the vegetables, reserving the stock, and put them on a warmed serving dish. Keep hot.

2 To make the sauce: melt the butter in a saucepan, add the flour and stir to form a smooth paste, or roux. Stir in the curry powder and ginger and stir over moderate heat for 3 minutes.

3 Gradually pour on the milk, orange juice and 300 ml/½ pint of the reserved stock, still stirring. Bring to the boil and simmer for 3 minutes. Taste the sauce and season with pepper, and salt if necessary. Remove the pan from the heat and stir in the cream.

4 Pour the sauce over the vegetables, lightly tossing them with a fork to coat them. Scatter with the almonds and chopped mint or parsley and serve on a bed of cooked rice.

Cook's Notes

TIME
The preparation of the vegetables will take about 10 minutes, and the cooking of the vegetables and sauce about 25 minutes altogether.

 FREEZING
Use 1 tablespoon cornflour in place of flour if you wish to freeze the sauce. It is best to freeze the vegetables and sauce separately.

 COOK'S TIP
To blanch almonds: boil for 30 seconds, then pinch off the skins.

● 240 calories/1000 kj per portion

Fresh tomato sauce

MAKES ABOUT 600 ML/1 PINT

750 g/1½ lb tomatoes, chopped (see Economy)
15 g/½ oz margarine or butter
1 tablespoon vegetable oil
2 onions, chopped
2 tablespoons tomato purée
1 teaspoon sugar
1 teaspoon salt
1 tablespoon chopped fresh parsley
½ teaspoon chopped fresh basil, or ¼ teaspoon dried basil
freshly ground black pepper

1 Heat the margarine and oil in a saucepan, add the onions and fry gently for 5 minutes until soft and lightly coloured.

2 Add the tomatoes and tomato purée, sugar, salt, parsley, basil and pepper to taste. Stir well, cover and let simmer gently for about 20 minutes until tomatoes are very soft and mushy. Remove from the heat and leave for about 10 minutes to cool slightly.

3 Pour the mixture into the goblet of a blender and work until smooth, then press through a sieve to remove tomato skins (alternatively, if you do not have a blender, work the sauce mixture through a sieve to purée it). ✳

4 Return the tomato sauce to the rinsed-out pan and reheat gently. Taste and adjust seasoning, if necessary, then serve as required (see Serving ideas).

Lamb kidneys in paprika sauce

SERVES 4

10 large lamb kidneys, skinned and halved
15 g/½ oz margarine or butter
3 tablespoons vegetable oil
1 onion, finely chopped
2 carrots, coarsely grated
25 g/1 oz plain flour
300 ml/½ pint chicken stock
1 tablespoon tomato purée
1-2 tablespoons sweet paprika, according to taste
salt and freshly ground black pepper

1 Remove the membrane and core from the kidneys, using kitchen scissors. Wash the kidneys and pat dry on absorbent paper, then cut each half into 4 pieces.

2 Heat the margarine and 1 table-spoon oil in a medium saucepan or flameproof casserole, add the kidneys and fry over high heat for about 5 minutes until they stiffen and turn colour, [!] stirring to prevent sticking. Transfer to a bowl

together with the juices and set aside.

3 Lower the heat to moderate, heat the remaining oil in the pan, then add the onion and fry gently for 5 minutes until soft and lightly coloured. Add the carrots and fry for 3-4 minutes until just tender, then sprinkle in the flour and continue cooking for 1 minute, stirring constantly.

4 Gradually stir in the chicken stock, with the tomato purée, 1 table-spoon paprika and salt and pepper to taste. Bring to the boil. Simmer for 1 minute, stirring constantly.

5 Add the kidneys to the sauce, cover and cook very gently for 5 minutes or until tender. Taste and add more paprika if wished. Transfer to a warmed serving dish and serve (see Serving ideas).

Cook's Notes

TIME
Total preparation and cooking time is 45 minutes.

WATCHPOINT
Boiling or overcooking the kidneys at this stage will toughen them.

SERVING IDEAS
Cook 225 g/8 oz pasta shapes, drain well and toss with 25 g/1 oz butter and 1 tablespoon finely chopped parsley. Arrange in a border around a hot serving dish and pour the prepared kidneys and sauce into the centre. Sprinkle with a little paprika pepper.

FREEZING
Transfer the kidneys and sauce to a rigid container, cool quickly, then seal, label and freeze for up to 2 months. To serve: reheat gently from frozen in a heavy-based saucepan until bubbling. Stir frequently, adding a little water if the kidneys stick to the bottom of the pan.

●315 calories/1325 kj per portion

Spaghetti with herby sauce

SERVES 4

500 g/1 lb spaghetti
2 tablespoons olive oil
1 medium onion, chopped
1 clove garlic, crushed (optional)
1 green pepper, deseeded and
  chopped
100 g/4 oz mushrooms, sliced
2 × 400 g/14 oz cans tomatoes
salt and freshly ground black pepper
25 g/1 oz margarine or butter
50 g/2 oz Parmesan cheese, grated
2 teaspoons Italian seasoning (see
  Did you know)

1 Heat the oil in a saucepan, add the onion, garlic, if using, green pepper and mushrooms and fry over moderate heat for about 10 minutes until softened, stirring occasionally.

2 Stir the tomatoes with their juice into the softened vegetables, breaking them up with a wooden spoon, and bring to the boil. Lower the heat, add salt and pepper to taste, then simmer for 20 minutes, stirring occasionally.

3 Meanwhile, cook the spaghetti in a large pan of boiling salted water for 10-12 minutes or until *al dente* (tender, yet firm to the bite).

4 Drain the spaghetti thoroughly, then return to the rinsed-out pan. Add the margarine, half the Parmesan, the Italian seasoning and salt and pepper to taste. Toss quickly until all the strands of spaghetti are coated, then transfer to a warmed serving dish.

5 Taste and adjust the seasoning of the herby sauce, then immediately pour over the spaghetti and mix well. Sprinkle with the remaining Parmesan and serve at once. Or if you prefer, hand the sauce separately.

Sweetbreads in tomato sauce

SERVES 4
750 g/1½ lb lamb sweetbreads
salt
75 g/3 oz margarine or butter
2 shallots, finely chopped
500 g/1 lb tomatoes, chopped
1 teaspoon freshly chopped
tarragon, or ½ teaspoon dried
tarragon
freshly ground black pepper

MARINADE
50 ml/2 fl oz lemon juice
1 tablespoon vegetable oil
2 tablespoons chopped parsley

TO SERVE
freshly cooked tagliatelle

1 Soak the sweetbreads in salted water for about 3½ hours, changing the water occasionally, until they turn white.
2 Meanwhile melt 25 g/1 oz margarine over moderate heat and cook the shallots until they are soft and transparent. Stir in the tomatoes and cook over very low heat for 10 minutes. Remove from the heat and leave to cool slightly, then work in a blender and sieve to remove tomato skins. If you do not have a blender, just press the mixture through a sieve. Stir in the tarragon and salt and pepper to taste. Set aside.
3 Drain the sweetbreads, then rinse them under cold running water. Blanch them by placing in a saucepan of fresh salted water and bringing quickly to the boil. Lower the heat and simmer for 3 minutes.
4 Drain and rinse the sweetbreads again, then peel away the skin and remove any stringy tissue and gristle. Set aside.
5 To make the marinade: mix together the lemon juice, oil, parsley and salt and pepper to taste. Place the sweetbreads in a bowl, then pour over the marinade. Mix well and leave for 30 minutes until cold.
6 Drain the sweetbreads on absorbent paper, pressing them firmly to flatten them and extract as much moisture as possible. Wipe dry, then slice thinly. Melt the remaining margarine in a frying-pan, add the sweetbreads and fry for 10-15 minutes until tender and lightly browned. Meanwhile reheat tomato sauce, and adjust seasoning.
7 Put freshly cooked tagliatelle in a serving dish and spoon the sweetbread and sauce into the centre.

Tagliatelle with sorrel sauce

SERVES 4
100 g/4 oz sorrel (see Buying guide)
25 g/1 oz butter
150 ml/¼ pint chicken stock
15 g/½ oz plain flour
150 ml/¼ pint double cream
freshly ground black pepper
little freshly grated nutmeg
salt
500 g/1 lb fresh tagliatelle
finely snipped chives, to garnish

1 Wash the sorrel well and remove any thick stalks. Dry the sorrel in a salad spinner, or leave to drain in a colander until dry.
2 Melt half the butter in a saucepan, add the sorrel leaves and stir over moderate heat for 4-5 minutes, until the sorrel is completely soft and reduced to a small mass.
3 Put the sorrel in a blender with the stock and blend until smooth.

4 Melt the remaining butter in the rinsed-out saucepan, sprinkle in the flour and stir over low heat for 1-2 minutes until straw-coloured. Gradually stir in sorrel and stock mixture and simmer, stirring, until smooth and well combined.
5 Remove from the heat, then stir in the cream and season to taste with pepper and nutmeg. Heat through without boiling.

6 Meanwhile, bring a large pan of salted water to the boil and cook the fresh tagliatelle for 5 minutes or until it is just tender but still firm to the bite (al dente).
7 Drain the pasta well, then return to the pan, pour the sauce over and toss until the pasta is evenly coated. Transfer to a warmed serving dish, sprinkle with snipped chives and serve at once.

Cook's Notes

 TIME
Only about 20 minutes to prepare the sauce and cook the fresh pasta.

 BUYING GUIDE
Sorrel is not often available in shops, but it is easy to grow from seed in the garden for harvesting in summer. If unobtainable, fresh spinach or watercress may be used as a substitute.

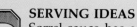 **SERVING IDEAS**
Sorrel sauce has a very subtle flavour which enhances mild-flavoured foods. Try it poured over fish kebabs or fish steaks, veal escalopes, boiled eggs or a simple French omelette.

This dish could be served as a starter followed by a light main course, or as a fresh tasting snack at any time.

●660 calories/2750 kj per portion

Peas portugaise

SERVES 4
500 g/1 lb frozen peas
2 tablespoons vegetable oil
1 medium onion, finely chopped
1 clove garlic, crushed (optional)
2 teaspoons sweet paprika
400 g/14 oz can tomatoes (see Variation)
1 teaspoon caster sugar
celery salt and freshly ground black pepper

1 Heat the oil in a saucepan, add the onion and garlic, if using, and fry over moderate heat for 3-4 minutes, stirring occasionally, until the onion is soft but not coloured. Stir in the paprika and cook for a further 2 minutes, then stir in the tomatoes with their juice, the sugar, celery salt and pepper to taste. Bring to the boil, lower the heat and simmer, uncovered, for about 10 minutes until the tomato sauce is reduced to a thick purée. ✳

2 Meanwhile, cook the peas in a small quantity of boiling salted water, according to packet directions. Drain well.

3 Turn the peas into a warmed serving dish. Taste and adjust the seasoning of the tomato sauce, then spoon it over the peas and fork through lightly so that the sauce can run through the peas to flavour them. Serve the peas at once, while very hot (See Serving ideas).

Sweet and sour sauce

SERVES 4

275-350 g/10-12 oz wholewheat
  spaghetti (see Cook's tips)
50 g/2 oz grated Parmesan
  cheese, to serve

SWEET AND SOUR SAUCE

750 g/1½ lb tomatoes, skinned and
  roughly chopped
25 g/1 oz butter
2 tablespoons olive or vegetable oil
2 onions, roughly chopped
1 clove garlic, crushed (optional)
225 ml/8 fl oz vegetable stock (see
  Buying guide)
65 g/2½ oz currants
2 teaspoons wine vinegar
1 teaspoon sugar
1 bay leaf
½ teaspoon dried basil
½ teaspoon dried thyme
¼ teaspoon ground cinnamon
salt and freshly ground black pepper

1 Make the sauce: heat the butter
and oil in a large saucepan, add the
onions and fry gently for 5 minutes
until soft and lightly coloured.

2 Add the remaining sauce
ingredients with salt and pepper to
taste. Bring to the boil then lower
the heat and simmer, uncovered, for
40-50 minutes, until thick, stirring
occasionally and breaking up the
tomato pieces with a wooden spoon
(see Cook's tips).

3 Bring a large pan of salted water to
the boil and cook the spaghetti for
15-20 minutes or until tender, yet
firm to the bite. Drain the spaghetti
thoroughly in a colander.

4 Divide the spaghetti between 4
warmed individual serving plates or
shallow soup bowls and top each
with a ladleful of the hot sauce.
Serve at once, with the grated
Parmesan cheese handed separately
in a small bowl.

Stuffed green peppers

SERVES 4
4 green peppers (see Buying guide)
150 g/5 oz long-grain rice
1 small onion, chopped
3 tablespoons vegetable oil
2 tablespoons tomato purée
5 tablespoons water
50 g/2 oz flaked almonds
50 g/2 oz sultanas
2 teaspoons dried oregano
grated zest of 1 orange
salt and freshly ground black pepper

1 Heat the oven to 180C/350F/Gas 4.
2 Bring a large saucepan of water to the boil, add the rice, bring back to the boil and cook for about 15 minutes until the rice is tender.
3 Meanwhile, slice the tops off the peppers and reserve them. Carefully remove the seeds from the peppers.
4 Drain the rice thoroughly, rinse under cold running water and then drain again.
5 In a bowl, thoroughly mix the rice together with all the remaining ingredients, reserving 2 tablespoons of the oil and 2 tablespoons of the water.
6 Fill the peppers with the stuffing mixture, packing it in well but taking care not to break the peppers.
7 Put the peppers into a casserole in which they will stand together closely but comfortably (see Cook's tip). Replace the tops.

8 Mix together the reserved oil and water and drizzle it over the peppers.

9 Cover the dish and bake for 25 minutes. Uncover for a further 25 minutes. Serve hot, warm or cold.

Cook's Notes

 TIME
Preparation takes about 30 minutes, including cooking the rice. Cooking in the oven takes 50 minutes.

 BUYING GUIDE
Buy firm, squat peppers as they stand up better in the dish and the stuffing will not fall out.

COOK'S TIP
If necessary, put a little crumpled foil between the peppers to keep them upright and remove it before serving.

 VARIATION
Red peppers could be used instead of green or use 2 of each.

 SERVING IDEAS
These make a tasty supper dish on their own or with a tomato sauce, served with hot garlic or pitta bread. They are especially good served warm. They could be served as a substantial starter, before a fairly light main course.

● 325 calories/1350 kj per portion

Creamy rigatoni

SERVES 4
500 g/1 lb rigatoni (see Buying
  guide)
salt
1 tablespoon vegetable oil
150 g/5 oz butter
100 g/4 oz button mushrooms,
  sliced
150 ml/¼ pint single cream
2 egg yolks
75 g/3 oz Parmesan cheese, grated
pinch of freshly grated nutmeg
freshly ground black pepper
100 g/4 oz frozen peas, cooked

1 Bring a large saucepan of salted water to the boil. Add the rigatoni and oil, lower the heat and simmer for about 12 minutes until just tender.
2 Meanwhile, melt 25 g/1 oz butter in a frying-pan. Add the mushrooms and fry over moderate heat until just tender. Set aside.
3 Make the sauce: melt the remaining butter in a large saucepan. Remove from the heat and set aside. In a bowl, quickly mix the cream, egg yolks and Parmesan with the nutmeg. Season with salt and plenty of pepper. Add this mixture to the melted butter in the pan and stir well.
4 When the rigatoni is nearly cooked, set the saucepan with the sauce mixture over very low heat to warm it through slightly. [!]
5 Drain the cooked rigatoni, add to the cream sauce with the peas and the mushrooms and stir continuously for a few seconds, then pile into warmed individual serving dishes and serve at once.

 Cook's Notes

 TIME
Preparation time is about 10 minutes, total cooking time 15 minutes.

[!] **WATCHPOINT**
When heating the cream mixture, watch it very carefully so that the eggs do not begin to scramble.

SERVING IDEAS
Serve as a supper or lunch dish with a tossed green salad. Offer extra Parmesan for sprinkling over the pasta.

 **BUYING GUIDE**
Rigatoni, a pasta that looks like large, ribbed macaroni, is available from delicatessens and some supermarkets. If it is difficult to obtain, use ordinary short-cut macaroni instead.

●870 calories/3650 kj per portion

Noodles
Chinese-style

SERVES 4

100 g/4 oz Chinese egg noodles (see
    Buying guide)
salt
2 tablespoons vegetable oil
6 spring onions, sliced
1 tablespoon grated fresh root
    ginger
500 g/1 lb Chinese leaves, cut into
    1 cm/½ inch thick slices
100 g/4 oz lean cooked ham,
    chopped (see Economy)
100 g/4 oz beansprouts
1 tablespoon soy sauce (see Buying
    guide)
4 tablespoons chicken stock, dry
    sherry or water
freshly ground black pepper

1 Bring a large saucepan of salted
water to the boil. Add the noodles,
bring back to the boil and cook for
about 3 minutes or according to
packet instructions, until just
tender. Drain and set aside.

Cook's Notes

TIME
10 minutes preparation,
10 minutes cooking.

ECONOMY
Any left-over lean
cooked meat can be
substituted for the ham.

SERVING IDEAS
This Chinese-style dish
is particularly good
served as a vegetable accompaniment to grilled or fried fish,
chops or chicken.
    To serve as a quick, econ-
omical light lunch or supper
dish, double the quantities. If
liked, add extra ingredients
such as sliced mushrooms or
cooked shelled prawns.

BUYING GUIDE
Thin Chinese egg
noodles are available at
supermarkets and delicatessens,
but if difficult to obtain, Italian
spaghetti or egg noodles can be
used instead. These will need
longer initial cooking in water—
follow packet instructions.
    Some supermarkets may have
a choice of soy sauces—choose
the lighter type for this dish.

● 230 calories/975 kj per portion

2 Heat the oil in a wok or large
frying-pan, add the onions and
ginger and fry gently for 2 minutes,
stirring constantly.
3 Add the Chinese leaves to the pan
with the chopped ham. Fry for a
further 2 minutes, stirring the
mixture constantly.
4 Add the drained noodles,
together with the beansprouts, soy
sauce, stock and salt and pepper to
taste. Increase the heat to moderate
and stir-fry for about 5 minutes until
the vegetables are tender but still
crisp and most of the liquid in the
pan has evaporated.
5 Taste and adjust seasoning. Turn
into a warmed serving dish.

Vegetable lasagne

SERVES 4

350 g/12 oz plain lasagne
2 tablespoons plus 1 teaspoon
   vegetable oil
2 onions, sliced
1 green pepper, deseeded and
   sliced
250 g/9 oz courgettes, sliced
250 g/9 oz mushrooms, sliced
400 g/14 oz can tomatoes
1 teaspoon dried mixed herbs
1 clove garlic, crushed (optional)
salt and freshly ground black pepper
3 tablespoons tomato purée
melted margarine, for greasing
1 fresh tomato, sliced

CHEESE SAUCE
50 g/2 oz margarine or butter
50 g/2 oz plain flour
600 ml/1 pint warm milk
250 g/9 oz Cheddar cheese, grated

1 Heat 2 tablespoons oil in a large heavy-based saucepan. Add the onions and fry over moderate heat for about 10 minutes until soft.

2 Add the green pepper and fry for another 2-3 minutes, then add the courgettes, mushrooms, tomatoes and their juice, herbs and garlic, if using. Add salt and pepper to taste, stir well, then simmer, uncovered, for 15 minutes, until vegetables are tender, stirring occasionally.

3 Stir in the tomato purée and cook for a further 15 minutes until the liquid has reduced and the mixture is thick. Taste and adjust seasoning.

4 Meanwhile, cook the lasagne: pour about 3 L/6 pints salted water into a very large saucepan with 1 teaspoon oil and bring to the boil. [!] Add the lasagne a piece at a time and boil rapidly, uncovered, for 15-20 minutes until just tender, stirring frequently. [!] Drain, rinse under cold running water, then leave to drain on absorbent paper.

5 Heat the oven to 200C/400F/Gas 6. Grease a 2 L/4 pint ovenproof dish or casserole with melted margarine.

6 Make the cheese sauce: melt the margarine in a small saucepan, sprinkle in the flour and stir over low heat for 1-2 minutes until straw-coloured. Remove from the heat and gradually stir in the milk. Return to the heat and simmer, stirring, until thick and smooth. Stir in half the cheese, with salt and pepper to taste.

7 Arrange the vegetable mixture, lasagne and cheese sauce in layers in the prepared dish, starting with the vegetable mixture and ending with cheese sauce. Sprinkle over the remaining cheese, top with tomato slices , and bake for 45 minutes until golden. Blot off excess oil with absorbent paper. Serve hot.

Cook's Notes

TIME
Preparation 45 minutes, cooking 45 minutes.

WATCHPOINTS
To add the lasagne to the boiling water, either bend it carefully or, if it is in long pieces, break them in half. The addition of the oil, and frequent stirring, are essential to prevent sticking.

FREEZING
Open freeze, turn out and foil wrap. Store for up to 3 months. To serve: bake from frozen in the original dish, allowing an extra 15-20 minutes cooking time.

SERVING IDEAS
Serve for lunch or supper with a salad of chicory, sweetcorn and mustard and cress in French dressing.

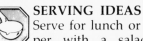

●935 calories/3900 kj per portion

Aubergine and pasta bake

SERVES 4

2 × 420 g/14¾ oz cans aubergines in sunflower seed oil (see Buying guide)
2 tablespoons vegetable oil
1 large onion, chopped
1 red pepper, deseeded and chopped
1 teaspoon dried mixed herbs
large pinch of ground cinnamon (see Cook's tips)
salt and freshly ground black pepper
175 g/6 oz wholewheat short-cut macaroni (see Variation)

TOPPING

2 eggs
300 ml/½ pint natural yoghurt
50 g/2 oz mature Cheddar cheese, grated
sweet paprika, for sprinkling

1 Heat the oven to 200C/400F/Gas 6.
2 Heat the oil in a heavy-based saucepan. Add the onion and red pepper and cook gently, stirring frequently, for about 10 minutes until the vegetables are softened. Stir in the aubergines and their oil, herbs, cinnamon and salt and pepper to taste. Cover and keep warm.
3 While the vegetables are cooking, bring a large pan of salted water to the boil. Add the macaroni and stir once. Bring the water back to the boil and cook for 9-11 minutes, until the macaroni is just tender.
4 Drain the macaroni thoroughly, then stir into the aubergine mixture. Check the seasoning, then turn into a 1.5-1.75 L/2½-3 pint baking or gratin dish and level the surface.
5 Make the topping: whisk the eggs into the yoghurt, then stir in the cheese and salt and pepper to taste. Pour over the aubergine mixture and sprinkle with paprika according to taste.
6 Bake in the oven for about 40 minutes, until the topping is set and browned (see Cook's tips). Serve hot, straight from the casserole.

Cook's Notes

TIME
30 minutes preparation, plus about 40 minutes baking time.

BUYING GUIDE
Canned aubergines, available in delicatessens and large supermarkets, are a useful buy when the fresh ones are not available.

● 700 calories/2925 kj per portion

VARIATION
Use white macaroni instead of wholewheat but remember that it needs less time to cook.

COOK'S TIPS
Cinnamon adds a hint of spice to the mixture, without making it 'sweet'.
The casserole can be left in the oven, with heat turned off, for 20-30 minutes without spoiling.

Chinese lettuce parcels

SERVES 6

6 large crisp lettuce leaves (see Preparation)
2 tablespoons vegetable oil
4 spring onions, finely chopped
1 teaspoon ground ginger
1 celery stalk, finely chopped
75 g/3 oz mushrooms, finely chopped
50 g/2 oz canned water chestnuts, drained and finely sliced
100 g/4 oz long-grain rice, cooked
100 g/4 oz frozen peas, cooked and drained
1½ tablespoons soy sauce
1 egg, beaten
extra soy sauce, to serve

1 Heat the oil in a wok or large frying-pan. Add the spring onions and ginger and fry gently for 2-3 minutes until soft.

2 Add the celery, mushrooms and water chestnuts and fry for a further 5 minutes.

3 Stir in the rice, peas and soy sauce. Remove the pan from the heat and stir in the egg.

4 Lay the lettuce leaves out flat on a work surface. Put about 2 generous tablespoons of the mixture at the base of each lettuce leaf. Fold the leaf around the mixture and roll up to form neat parcels. Secure with cocktail sticks, if necessary.

5 Place the parcels in a steamer. If you do not have a steamer, use a metal colander which fits neatly inside a saucepan (the base must not touch the water). Fill the pan with boiling water, place the parcels in the colander and place the colander in the pan. Cover with foil or lid of steamer and steam for 5 minutes.

6 Remove the cocktail sticks from the parcels, if using, then place the parcels on a warmed serving dish. Serve at once, as a starter or snack, with extra soy sauce handed separately.

Hot beans and rice

SERVES 4-6

425 g/15 oz can red kidney beans,
  drained
250 g/9 oz long-grain rice
2 tablespoons vegetable oil
1 onion, finely chopped
1 clove garlic, crushed (optional)
1 red pepper, deseeded and thinly
  sliced
1 green pepper, deseeded and
  thinly sliced
2 celery stalks, finely chopped
2 large tomatoes, skinned,
  deseeded and chopped
1 tablespoon sweet paprika
1 teaspoon cayenne pepper
freshly ground black pepper
600 ml/1 pint water
salt
celery leaves, to garnish

1 Heat the oil in a heavy-based saucepan, add the onion and garlic, if using, and fry gently for 5 minutes until soft and lightly coloured.

2 Add the sliced red and green peppers and celery and fry for a further 3 minutes. Add the tomatoes, drained beans, rice, paprika, cayenne and black pepper. Stir and cook for a further minute.

Pour in the water, stir the mixture well and bring to the boil.

3 Cover and simmer gently for 25 minutes until the rice is tender and all the liquid has been absorbed. Season with salt and pepper to taste.

4 Spoon the mixture into a warmed serving dish, garnish with the celery leaves and serve the bean and rice salad at once.

Cook's Notes

 TIME
Preparation takes about 20 minutes, final cooking takes 25 minutes.

 SERVING IDEAS
This substantial dish goes particularly well with grilled or barbecued meat. To serve cold as a salad, allow to cool, then toss in an oil and vinegar dressing.

VARIATIONS
Use 250 g/9 oz dried kidney beans instead of the canned type. Soak the beans overnight, then put them in a pan and cover with fresh water. Boil briskly for at least 10 minutes then simmer gently for 1½-2 hours. Drain and proceed with the recipe.

● 395 calories/1650 kj per portion

Stuffed cabbage pie

SERVES 4-6

1 green cabbage, weighing about
    1 kg/2 lb
175 g/6 oz long-grain rice
salt
15 g/½ oz margarine or butter
1 onion, chopped
1 cooking apple, weighing about
    150 g/5 oz
50 g/2 oz stoned dates, chopped
1 orange (see Preparation)
75 g/3 oz Cheddar cheese, grated
1 egg, beaten
freshly ground black
    pepper
margarine, for greasing

1 Heat the oven to 180C/350F/Gas 4
and grease an ovenproof dish 20 cm/
8 inches in diameter and 7.5 cm/3
inches deep.

2 Bring a pan of salted water to the
boil and cook the rice for about 10
minutes until just tender.

3 Meanwhile, remove about 8 outer
leaves of the cabbage and cut off any
thick hard midribs. Bring another
pan of salted water to the boil and
blanch the cabbage leaves for 4
minutes. Drain and set aside. Chop
the remaining cabbage and reserve.

4 Melt the margarine in a large
saucepan, add the onion and fry
gently for 5 minutes until soft.

5 Add the chopped cabbage to the
pan and cook over moderate heat,
stirring, for 5 minutes. Peel, core
and chop the apple and add to the
pan. Cook for a further minute.

6 Drain the rice thoroughly and add
to the pan with the dates, orange
zest and juice. Remove from heat.

7 Line the base and sides of the dish
with half the blanched cabbage
leaves, arranging them so that they
overlap and allowing them to
overhang the dish. Stir the cheese
and egg into the rice mixture,
season to taste with salt and pepper,
then spoon into the lined dish.
Level the surface of the mixture and
cover with the remaining leaves.
Fold over overhanging leaves.

8 Cover the dish tightly with foil
and cook for 45 minutes.

9 Loosen the sides with a knife and
turn out on to a warmed plate.

Cook's Notes

 TIME
45 minutes preparation,
including boiling the
rice and blanching the leaves,
then 45 minutes in the oven.

 PREPARATION
Grate the zest of half
the orange and squeeze
the juice from the whole orange.

● 370 calories/1560 kj per portion

 SERVING IDEAS
Serve as an accompani-
ment to meat dishes, as
a starter or as a complete
vegetarian meal with a
home-made tomato sauce
poured over the top.

 VARIATION
Use soaked dried apri-
cots or drained canned
apricots instead of the dates.

Vegetable fried rice

SERVES 4
250 g/9 oz long-grain rice
salt
250 g/9 oz carrots, diced
1 parsnip, diced
1 small turnip, diced
2 tablespoons vegetable oil
1 large onion, chopped
1 clove garlic, crushed (optional)
50 g/2 oz button mushrooms, sliced
2 large tomatoes, skinned and sliced
50 g/2 oz frozen peas, defrosted
freshly ground black pepper
2 eggs, lightly beaten
1 tablespoon chopped fresh parsley
grated Parmesan cheese, to serve

1 Bring a large saucepan of salted water to the boil, add the rice and cover. Lower the heat and simmer for 10 minutes, or until the rice is just tender.
2 Meanwhile, bring another pan of salted water to the boil. Add the carrots, parsnip and turnip and cover. Lower the heat and cook for about 8-10 minutes, or until all the

vegetables are barely tender.
3 Drain the cooked root vegetables and reserve. Drain the rice in a colander and rinse well under hot running water to separate the grains. Drain again.
4 Heat the oil in a large non-stick saucepan, add the onion and garlic, if using, and fry gently for 5 minutes, until the onion is soft and lightly coloured.
5 Add the drained root vegetables

to the pan, together with the mushrooms, tomatoes, peas and rice. Stir well and season to taste with salt and plenty of pepper. Cover the pan and cook over very low heat for 10 minutes.
6 Stir in the eggs and gently turn the mixture so that the egg cooks. Remove from the heat and turn into a warmed serving dish. Garnish with the parsley and serve at once with the Parmesan cheese.

Cook's Notes

 TIME
This dish will take about 35 minutes to make.

VARIATIONS
Small, partly-cooked cauliflower florets or broccoli make tasty alternatives to the root vegetables used here—and their shape adds a pleasant variation, too.
Make the dish even more substantial by adding about 100 g/ 4 oz chopped ham or cooked chicken at the beginning of stage 5.

FREEZING
Cool completely and pack into a rigid container. Seal, label and freeze for up to 2 months. To serve: allow to defrost overnight in the refrigerator. Reheat very gently and stir in the eggs just before serving.

SERVING IDEAS
This dish makes an excellent accompaniment to meat dishes. Or serve with tomato sauce on its own.

● 410 calories/1735 kj per portion

Rice-stuffed courgettes

SERVES 4

4 courgettes
1 tablespoon vegetable oil
1 onion, finely chopped
250 g/9 oz chicken livers, chopped
175 g/6 oz cooked long-grain rice
   (see Cook's tip)
2 tomatoes, chopped
2 tablespoons chopped parsley
pinch of thyme
1 teaspoon lemon juice
salt and freshly ground black pepper
green and red pepper rings
sprigs of fresh thyme and parsley
   and lemon twist, to garnish
margarine, for greasing

1 Heat the oven to 190C/375F/Gas 5. Grease an ovenproof dish.
2 Cut the courgettes in half lengthways and scoop out the seeds. Arrange in a single layer in the prepared dish.
3 Make the stuffing: heat the oil in a saucepan. Add the onion and fry gently for 5 minutes until soft and lightly coloured. Add the chicken livers and fry for a further 5 minutes, stirring, until evenly browned. Remove pan from heat.
4 Add rice, tomatoes, herbs and lemon juice and mix well. Season to taste with salt and pepper.

5 Spoon the stuffing into each courgette half, pressing it down firmly with the back of a spoon.
6 Cover the dish with greased foil and cook in the oven for 35-40 minutes, until the courgettes are tender. Serve hot on a bed of pepper rings, garnished with herbs and a lemon twist.

Cook's Notes

 TIME
Preparation takes about 25 minutes and cooking takes 35-40 minutes.

SERVING IDEAS
Stuffed courgettes are very good on their own for a light lunch. Alternatively, for a more substantial dish serve with gravy or tomato sauce and mixed vegetables.

 COOK'S TIP
For this amount of cooked rice you will need 50 g/2 oz raw rice.

VARIATIONS
The stuffing also makes a delicious filling for marrow: cut a small marrow into slices crossways and remove the seeds. Place the slices in a single layer in an ovenproof dish and fill the centre hollows with the stuffing. There should be enough for 4 marrow slices.
Use turkey or lamb liver instead of chicken livers.
Alternatively, use lean cooked ham and replace the tomatoes with mushrooms.

●190 calories/1800 kj per portion

Spinach and sage rice

SERVES 4
250 g/9 oz spinach, stalks and
    midribs removed, finely chopped
    (see Watchpoint)
2 tablespoons vegetable oil
1 small onion, finely chopped
1 tablespoon lemon juice
½ teaspoon powdered dried sage
1½ teaspoons salt
freshly ground black pepper
250 g/9 oz long-grain rice
500 ml/18 fl oz boiling water
25 g/1 oz Cheshire cheese, crumbled

1 Heat the oil in a medium saucepan and add the spinach, onion,
lemon juice, sage, ½ teaspoon of the
salt and plenty of freshly ground
black pepper. Cook over moderate
heat for 5 minutes, stirring constantly until the spinach is soft and
the mixture is fairly dry.
2 Lower the heat, add the rice to the
pan and cook gently for a further 2
minutes, stirring. Pour in the boiling water, add the remaining salt
and bring back to the boil. Stir once,
then lower the heat, cover the pan
and cook very gently for 20 minutes,
until the rice is cooked and the
liquid has been absorbed.
3 Stir the mixture, turn it into a
warmed serving dish, sprinkle with
cheese and serve at once as an
accompaniment to meat dishes,
particularly pork.

Cook's Notes

TIME
20 minutes preparation,
30 minutes cooking.

WATCHPOINT
After . washing the
spinach it is important
to dry it thoroughly, a leaf at a
time, in a clean tea-towel, otherwise it will make the rice too wet
and spoil the dish.

VARIATIONS
The garnish of crumbled
Cheshire cheese can be
replaced by any other type of
crumbled or grated cheese.
Sliced tomatoes or halved,
stoned olives make an attractive
additional garnish, adding
colour to the dish.

●330 calories/1375 kj per portion

Chicken and pasta salad

SERVES 4

350 g/12 oz cooked chicken, cubed
150 g/5 oz pasta shells
salt
1 teaspoon vegetable oil
150 ml/¼ pint soured cream
1 tablespoon capers
2 spring onions, chopped
1 tablespoon chopped fresh
tarragon (see Variations)
salt and freshly ground black pepper
a little extra chopped tarragon, to
garnish

1 Bring a large pan of salted water to the boil, swirl in the oil, then add the pasta. Bring back to the boil and cook for 7-10 minutes until tender.
2 Drain thoroughly, then rinse under cold running water to remove excess starch (see Cook's tip). Drain again and set aside until cold.

3 Mix all the other ingredients together thoroughly, with salt and pepper to taste and then stir in the pasta shells. Turn into a deep serving bowl, garnish with a sprinkling of tarragon. Serve cold.

Cook's Notes

TIME
Total preparation takes about 20 minutes.

SERVING IDEAS
Serve with a simple green or tomato salad.

COOK'S TIP
Rinsing the pasta under cold water also prevents it sticking together when cold.

VARIATIONS
If fresh tarragon is not available, use another fresh herb such as mint, parsley or chives.
For a more substantial dish, add a quartered hard-boiled egg per person.
Cold cooked fish may be used instead of cooked chicken.

● 325 calories/1350 kj per portion

Pasta salad

SERVES 4
250 g/9 oz green tagliatelle
salt
45 g/1¾ oz can anchovy fillets,
  drained and soaked in milk
  for 20 minutes
225 g/8 oz Cheddar cheese, finely
  diced
2 tomatoes, skinned and thickly
  sliced
2 celery stalks, chopped
8 black olives, halved and stoned
2 tablespoons grated Parmesan
  cheese

DRESSING
3 tablespoons vegetable oil
1 tablespoon wine vinegar
½ teaspoon mustard powder
freshly ground black pepper

1 Cook the tagliatelle in boiling salted water for 5-10 minutes until just tender. ⚠ Drain thoroughly, then rinse well under cold running water, to remove any excess starch from the pasta.
2 While the pasta is cooking, make the dressing: combine the oil, vinegar, mustard and salt and pepper to taste in a screw-top jar. Shake the jar well until all the ingredients in the dressing are thoroughly blended.
3 Drain the anchovy fillets and pat dry with absorbent paper. Put them into a bowl with cooked tagliatelle, cheese, tomatoes, celery, and olives, then pour in the dressing. Toss gently, until all the salad ingredients are evenly coated.
4 Pile the salad on to a serving dish and sprinkle the Parmesan cheese over the top.

Cook's Notes

TIME
This salad takes about 20 minutes; including the cooking of the tagliatelle.

SERVING IDEAS
Serve this tasty salad as a lunch or supper dish with a green salad and some hot garlic bread.

VARIATION
Other pasta shapes, such as shells or short tubes, can be used.

WATCHPOINT
It is very important not to overcook the pasta, or the salad will be stodgy.

●600 calories/2500 kj per portion

Tropicana salad

SERVES 4-6
75 g/3 oz pasta shapes
2 grapefruits, peeled and segmented
2 oranges, peeled and segmented
2 large dessert apples, diced
3 celery stalks, finely chopped
100 g/4 oz salami, skinned and
    roughly chopped
1 tablespoon snipped chives
25 g/1 oz salted cashew nuts

DRESSING
4 tablespoons thick bottled
    mayonnaise
2 tablespoons fresh orange juice
finely grated zest and juice of 1
    lemon
2 tablespoons rosehip syrup
salt and freshly ground black pepper

TO GARNISH
slices of unpeeled orange
watercress

1 Bring a pan of salted water to the
boil and cook the pasta for about 10
minutes or until just tender. Rinse
in cold water and drain well.
2 Turn the pasta into a large bowl
and stir in the prepared fruit, celery
and salami. Mix thoroughly.
3 To make the dressing: mix
together the mayonnaise, orange
juice, lemon zest and juice and the
rosehip syrup. Whisk with a fork
until thoroughly combined. Season
with salt and pepper.
4 Toss the salad and dressing well
together, then turn into a salad bowl
and sprinkle over the chives and
cashews.
5 Serve garnished with slices of
unpeeled orange and watercress.

Cook's Notes

TIME
Preparation of this salad
takes 20 minutes plus 10
minutes to cook the pasta.

SERVING IDEAS
This makes a refreshing
summer lunch.

●430 calories/1800 kj per portion

Hot pasta and sausage salad

SERVES 4
175 g/6 oz pasta shells
250 g/9 oz garlic sausage, skinned
    and cut into 1 cm/½ inch cubes
salt
2 teaspoons vegetable oil
25 g/1 oz quick dried peas
1 small red pepper, deseeded and
    cut into strips
150 ml/¼ pint soured cream
2 tablespoons chopped fresh
    parsley
freshly ground black pepper

1 Bring a saucepan of salted water
to the boil, add the oil, pasta and
peas and then cook for 7-8 minutes.
2 Add the sausage and red pepper
to the pan and continue cooking for
a further 5 minutes until the pasta is
just cooked.
3 Drain the mixture well, return to
the rinsed-out pan and stir in the
soured cream, parsley and salt and
pepper to taste. Heat through very
gently. Transfer the pasta and
sausage to a warmed serving dish
and serve at once.

Cook's Notes

 TIME
Preparation and cooking
take about 25 minutes.

 VARIATIONS
Use 100 g/4 oz frozen
peas instead of dried,
but only cook them for 3-4
minutes. Instead of garlic
sausage, use fresh cooked or
drained canned sausages or any
variety of frankfurters.

 SERVING IDEAS
Serve hot with buttered
brown bread or toast
and a green salad.

 COOK'S TIP
Pasta shells look
attractive because of
their shape but you can use any
other small pasta shapes.

●420 calories/1750 kj per portion

Radish and pasta salad

SERVES 4
250 g/9 oz radishes
100 g/4 oz pasta spirals or pasta
  shells
salt
1 teaspoon vegetable oil
2 tablespoons snipped chives
150 ml/¼ pint soured cream
freshly ground black pepper

1 Bring a large pan of salted water to the boil, swirl in the oil, then add the pasta. Bring back to the boil and cook, uncovered, for 10-15 minutes until tender but firm to the bite. Drain the pasta thoroughly in a colander, then rinse well under cold running water, to remove any excess starch and to cool down the pasta. Drain again thoroughly and leave on one side.

2 Trim the top and bottom of the radishes and cut into 3-4 slices.

3 Transfer the pasta to a serving dish and add the radishes, chives, soured cream and salt and pepper to taste. Toss the salad well and serve at once, while still fresh.

Lamb and mint pasta salad

SERVES 4
350-500 g/12 oz-1 lb cooked lamb, sliced
salt
1 teaspoon vegetable oil
250 g/9 oz pasta rings (see Buying guide)
1 large onion, sliced
mint sprigs, to garnish

MINT DRESSING
2 tablespoons chopped fresh mint
2 tablespoons capers, finely chopped
2 tablespoons vegetable oil
4½ teaspoons white wine vinegar
2 teaspoons caster sugar
good pinch of mustard powder
freshly ground black pepper

1 Bring a pan of salted water to the boil, swirl in the oil and add the pasta. Cook for 5 minutes, then add the onion slices and cook for a further 5 minutes until the pasta is tender but firm to the bite.

2 Meanwhile, make the dressing: put the chopped mint into a large bowl with the capers, oil, vinegar, sugar and mustard. Season to taste with salt and pepper and beat to mix well together.

3 Drain the pasta and onion, rinse under cold running water, then drain again very thoroughly. Add to the mint and caper dressing and stir well until the pasta and onion are evenly coated.

4 Arrange the cooked lamb in the centre of a large serving platter, spoon the pasta salad around the meat and then garnish with mint sprigs. Serve the dish at once (see Serving ideas).

Curried rice salad

SERVES 6

100 g/4 oz medium-grain or Italian rice
salt
175 g/6 oz can pimientos, drained
1 green pepper, deseeded and chopped
2 tomatoes, skinned, deseeded and chopped
2 spring onions, thinly sliced
2 tablespoons blanched almonds, roughly chopped
4 tablespoons canned sweetcorn, drained
1 tablespoon seedless raisins
1 tablespoon sultanas
margarine or butter, for greasing
watercress sprigs, to garnish

DRESSING

5 tablespoons olive oil
1 tablespoon red wine vinegar
2 teaspoons lemon juice
1 clove garlic, crushed (optional)
1 teaspoon caster sugar
1 teaspoon mild curry powder

1 Cook the rice in a large pan of boiling salted water for 10-12 minutes, until it is just tender. Drain the rice in a colander, rinse under cold running water, drain again and turn into a large bowl.
2 Chop one of the canned pimientos. Cut the remaining ones into long strips about 1 cm/½ inch thick and reserve for the garnish.
3 Stir the chopped pimiento into the rice, together with the green pepper, tomatoes, spring onions, almonds, sweetcorn, raisins and sultanas. Mix well together so that the vegetables and fruit are distributed evenly.
4 Make the dressing: put all the dressing ingredients into a screw-top jar, add salt to taste and shake well. Mix the dressing into the rice mixture.
5 Pack the rice mixture into a 600 ml/1 pint bowl, pushing it firmly down with the back of a large spoon. Cover the bowl with cling film and set aside to cool.
6 Unmould the rice salad on to a plate (see Cook's tip). Arrange pimiento on the top in a wheel pattern and garnish with watercress. Serve with any cold meat.

Cook's Notes

 TIME
Total preparation and cooking time is 30 minutes.

 COOK'S TIP
To unmould the rice salad, run a thin-bladed knife around the inside of the bowl to loosen it. Put a flat serving plate over the bowl and, holding the two firmly together, invert the bowl. Give a sharp shake to release the rice mould. Stand the plate on a surface and gently lift off the bowl, taking care not to damage the mould.

 PREPARATION
To skin the tomatoes, cover them with boiling water and leave for 1 minute; then plunge into cold water. Stab a tomato with a fork, remove from the water and peel away the skin with a sharp knife. Repeat with the others.

●215 calories/900 kj per portion

Brown rice ring

SERVES 4

150 g/5 oz brown rice
salt
1 red pepper, deseeded and diced
(see Preparation)
1 green pepper, deseeded and
diced
25 g/1 oz margarine or butter
1 Spanish onion, chopped
250 g/9 oz tomatoes, skinned,
deseeded and chopped
½ small cucumber, diced (see
Cook's tip)

DRESSING

3 tablespoons vegetable oil
1 teaspoon wine vinegar or lemon
juice
pinch of mustard powder
pinch of caster sugar
salt and freshly ground black pepper

1 Rinse the rice and put it into a
large saucepan of boiling salted
water. Bring to the boil again,
reduce heat and simmer, very
gently, for about 40 minutes, until
the rice is cooked and has absorbed
all the water. ! If necessary, add
more boiling water during cooking.
Rinse under cold running water and
leave in a sieve to drain thoroughly.
2 Meanwhile, soften the diced
peppers slightly by plunging them
into boiling water for 30 seconds.
Drain and refresh immediately
under cold running water.
3 Melt the margarine in a frying-
pan, add the onion and cook over
gentle heat for 5 minutes until it is
soft and translucent. Remove from
the heat and stir in the peppers,
tomatoes and cucumber.
4 Put the ingredients for the
dressing in a large bowl and whisk
with a fork to blend thoroughly.
5 Add the drained rice to the
dressing with the vegetables and
gently mix all the ingredients
together, using 2 forks. Pack into a
850 ml/1½ pint plain ring mould
and refrigerate for at least 1 hour.
6 To unmould: run a knife around
the ring mould. Invert a serving
plate on top and give the mould a
sharp tap. Serve chilled.

Chicken and courgette salad

SERVES 4

350 g/12 oz boneless cooked
   chicken meat, cut into
   bite-sized pieces
250 g/9 oz long-grain rice
2 tablespoons vegetable oil
350 g/12 oz courgettes, thickly
   sliced
2 teaspoons curry powder
1½ tablespoons lemon juice
salt and freshly ground black pepper
2 tablespoons thick bottled
   mayonnaise
2 bananas

1 Bring a pan of salted water to the boil and cook the rice for 12-15 minutes until just tender. Rinse well under cold running water to separate the grains. Drain well and set aside for 30 minutes until cold.
2 Meanwhile, heat half the oil in a frying-pan and fry courgettes and curry powder briskly for about 4-5 minutes, turning, until golden and cooked through. Remove from pan with a slotted spoon and drain.
3 Put 1 tablespoon of the lemon juice and the remaining oil in a large serving bowl, season to taste with salt and pepper and mix well. Stir in the cold rice and courgettes.
4 Put mayonnaise into a separate bowl. Add the cooked chicken pieces and stir them into the mayonnaise until well coated.
5 Fold the chicken into the rice mixture until evenly distributed. Peel and slice the bananas and arrange on top, then sprinkle with the remaining lemon juice. Serve at once (see Serving ideas).

Cook's Notes

 TIME
Total preparation and cooking time for the dish is 1 hour.

WATCHPOINT
The courgettes should be only just tender; if they are overcooked and too soft they will break up and spoil the appearance of the salad.

SERVING IDEAS
Sprinkle this hearty salad with a little lightly toasted shredded coconut and garnish with a border of lemon slices.

 VARIATIONS
Use chunks of cooked ham instead of chicken and, if liked, add chopped, well-drained canned pineapple segments.

●515 calories/2150 kj per portion

Turkey and ham salad

SERVES 4
175 g/6 oz cooked turkey, cut into
    bite-sized pieces
250 g/9 oz cooked ham, diced
250 g/9 oz long-grain rice
salt
1 small red pepper, deseeded and
    chopped
5 spring onions, chopped
4 tablespoons thick bottled
    mayonnaise
3 tablespoons natural yoghurt
1 clove garlic, crushed (optional)
freshly ground black pepper
100 g/4 oz grapes, halved, pips
    removed
3 ripe kiwifruit, peeled and sliced
    (see Buying guide and
    Preparation)
lettuce or chicory leaves, to serve

1 Cook the rice in plenty of boiling
salted water for 12-15 minutes until
tender, then rinse well under cold
running water to separate the
grains.
2 Put the drained rice into a large
bowl, add the turkey, ham, pepper
and spring onions and fold in gently.

3 In a small bowl, mix together the
mayonnaise, yoghurt and garlic, if
using, and season with salt and
pepper. Pour over the rice mixture
and fold to mix again.

4 Gently stir the grapes and kiwifruit into the salad. Cover and
keep in a cool place until required.
5 To serve: pile the salad on a bed of
lettuce.

Greek rice ring

SERVES 4

175 g/6 oz long-grain rice
100 g/4 oz small black olives,
    stoned
salt
100 g/4 oz left-over cooked lamb,
    diced
50 g/2 oz stuffed green olives,
    sliced
2 tomatoes, diced
1 green pepper, deseeded and cut
    into 1 cm/½ inch pieces (see
    Cook's tips)
2 tablespoons olive oil
1 tablespoon lemon juice
1 teaspoon chopped fresh mint
½ teaspoon dried oregano
freshly ground black pepper
margarine, for greasing

1 Heat the oven to 180C/350F/Gas 4.
2 Lightly grease an 850 ml/1½ pint ring mould (see Cook's tips) and arrange the black olives on the base.
3 Bring a pan of salted water to the boil and cook the rice for 15 minutes or until it is tender but still firm to the bite. Drain well, but do not rinse as the starch is necessary to hold the rice together.
4 Put the rice into a large bowl and mix thoroughly with the remaining ingredients. Season.
5 Spoon mixture into prepared ring mould and press down lightly. Cover with greased foil, then bake in the oven for 25 minutes. Turn out on to a warmed serving platter and serve at once (see Serving ideas).

Cook's Notes

TIME
Preparation time is about 15 minutes and cooking time 45-50 minutes.

COOK'S TIPS
If pepper pieces are any larger, they may cause ring to break up when unmoulded.

If a ring mould is unavailable, use a 18 cm/7 inch solid-based round cake tin instead.

VARIATIONS
Instead of lamb, use left-over chicken.

FOR CHILDREN
If they do not like the flavour of olives, omit both black and green olives and add 100 g/4 oz cooked peas to the rice instead.

SERVING IDEAS
Serve hot on its own, or leave to cool and serve cold. For a buffet lunch, serve with a Greek salad of Feta cheese, onions and tomatoes piled in the centre of the rice ring.

●305 calories/1275 kj per portion

Mediterranean rice dessert

SERVES 4
450 g/15½ oz can creamed rice milk pudding
1 tablespoon cornflour
150 ml/¼ pint milk
2 tablespoons sugar
1 large egg yolk
grated zest of 1 small lemon
grated chocolate, to decorate

1 Turn the creamed rice into a saucepan and set over low heat.
2 Blend the cornflour with 2-3 tablespoons of milk, then stir in half the remaining milk. Add the cornflour mixture to the rice together with the sugar. Bring slowly to the boil, stirring, and simmer for 2 minutes.
3 Beat the egg yolk with the remaining milk, then stir into the rice pudding. Add the lemon zest and simmer, stirring, for 2 minutes more.
4 Remove the pan from the heat and pour the pudding into 4 individual dessert bowls. Sprinkle a little grated chocolate over each pudding. Serve hot or chilled.

Cook's Notes

TIME
Preparation and cooking take about 10 minutes. Remember to allow chilling time if serving cold.

ECONOMY
This is a quick and easy way to stretch a can of rice pudding to serve 4.

DID YOU KNOW
This type of pudding is popular in the Mediterranean, where it is often sprinkled with cinnamon.

●185 calories/775 kj per portion

Polish noodle dessert

SERVES 4-6
225 g/8 oz tagliatelle (see Buying guide)
3 tablespoons poppy seeds (see Economy)
2 tablespoons clear honey
½ teaspoon vanilla flavouring
salt
2 tablespoons melted butter
175 g/6 oz sultanas or seedless raisins

1 Put the poppy seeds into a bowl, cover with boiling water and leave to soak for 3 hours.
2 Drain the poppy seeds in a fine sieve, then press gently to extract as much liquid as possible. Spread the poppy seeds over a clean tea-towel and pat dry.
3 Put the poppy seeds into a large bowl. Add the honey and vanilla and mash together with a wooden spoon to make a thick black paste.
4 Bring a large pan of salted water to the boil, add the tagliatelle and stir once. Bring back to the boil and cook for about 7 minutes, until the tagliatelle is *al dente* (tender, yet firm to the bite). Drain well.
5 Add the tagliatelle to the poppy seed paste with the melted butter and sultanas. Mix together well and serve at once (see Serving ideas).

Imperial rice mould

SERVES 6

4 cubes of a tablet red jelly,
    dissolved in 150 ml/¼ pint
    boiling water and cooled
1 rounded tablespoon (1 sachet)
    powdered gelatine
3 tablespoons water
825 g/1 lb 13 oz can creamed rice
    pudding, warmed
3-4 drops vanilla flavouring
50 g/2 oz glacé cherries, quartered
25 g/1 oz sultanas
15 g/½ oz angelica, chopped
2 egg whites
150 ml/¼ pint whipping or double
    cream

1 Rinse out a 1.5 L/2½ pint metal
jelly mould with cold water, then
shake off the excess moisture.
Spoon the jelly into the mould,
cover and refrigerate until set.
2 Meanwhile, sprinkle the gelatine
over the water in a small heatproof
bowl and leave to soak for 5 minutes
until spongy. Stand the bowl in a
pan of gently simmering water for
1-2 minutes, stirring occasionally,
until the gelatine has dissolved.
3 Stir the gelatine into the warm
rice pudding, then stir in the
vanilla, cherries, sultanas and
angelica. Turn the mixture into a
clean bowl, cover and chill in the
refrigerator, stirring occasionally,
until on the point of setting. ⚠
4 In a clean, dry bowl, whisk the
egg whites until standing in stiff
peaks. Whip the cream until it forms
soft peaks. Using a large metal
spoon, fold the cream and then the
egg whites into the rice mixture.
5 Spoon the mixture into the
mould, over the jelly, cover and
return to the refrigerator for 2-3
hours, until set (see Cook's tip).
6 Unmould the dessert. Loosen
edges with a palette knife then dip
mould in hot water for 1-2 seconds.
Invert a dampened plate on top
then, holding mould and plate
together, invert them giving a sharp
shake halfway round. Lift off mould
and mop up any liquid from plate.
Leave at room temperature for 30
minutes, to take the chill off the
flavour, before serving.

Cook's Notes

TIME
40 minutes preparation,
plus setting time.

SPECIAL OCCASION
Spoon half the red jelly
into the mould and chill
until on the point of setting.
Press slices of banana and
'diamonds' of angelica into the
almost-set jelly in a decorative
pattern. Spoon over the remaining jelly and return to the
refrigerator to set.

COOK'S TIP
The dessert can be pre-
pared ahead up to the
end of stage 5 and kept, covered,
in the refrigerator for up to 24
hours.

WATCHPOINT
Do not let the mixture
become too stiff, or it
will be difficult to incorporate
the egg whites and cream.

●310 calories/1300 kj per portion

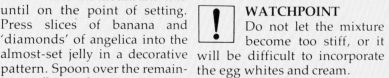

Date rice

proof pie dish and place the dish on a baking sheet.

3 Bake in the oven for about 2 hours, or until the rice is tender and most of the milk has been absorbed. Serve hot (see Serving ideas).

SERVES 4
50 g/2 oz pudding rice
600 ml/1 pint milk
15 g/½ oz margarine or butter
50 g/2 oz pressed dates, chopped
(see Buying guide)
grated zest of 1 orange
melted margarine, for greasing

1 Heat the oven to 150C/300F/Gas 2. Brush the inside of an 850 ml/1½ pint ovenproof pie dish with melted margarine.

2 Put the rice, milk and margarine into a saucepan. Bring just to boiling point, then remove from the heat. Stir in the dates and orange zest. Pour into the prepared oven-

Cook's Notes

 TIME
Preparation 20 minutes, cooking time 2 hours.

ECONOMY
If you are using the oven heated to 170C/325F/ Gas 3 for a main dish, the pudding may be baked on the bottom shelf.

 VARIATIONS
Use other dried fruits, such as raisins or sultanas in place of some or all of the dates. For added flavour, grate a little nutmeg over the top.

 BUYING GUIDE
Buy dates that are already stoned—available from most supermarkets.

SERVING IDEAS
Serve hot, topped with chilled fresh orange segments, or drained, canned mandarins.

 COOK'S TIP
Heating the milk and rice first helps to keep baking time to a minimum.

● 220 calories/925 kj per portion

Rich rice pudding

SERVES 4
100 g/4 oz pudding rice
600 ml/1 pint milk
finely grated zest of ½ orange
75 g/3 oz caster sugar
25 g/1 oz butter
3 egg yolks, beaten
150 ml/¼ pint single cream
butter, for greasing

1 Heat the oven to 180C/350F/Gas 4. Generously butter a 1.25 L/2 pint ovenproof dish (see Cook's tip).

2 Put the rice in a saucepan with the milk and orange zest and bring slowly to the boil. Cook, stirring occasionally, for 15-20 minutes, until the rice is just tender.

3 Turn the heat off under the rice, add the caster sugar and butter and stir until melted. Allow the rice mixture to cool for 5 minutes. Thoroughly stir in the beaten egg yolks, followed by the cream.

4 Pour into the prepared dish and bake in the oven for about 40 minutes, stirring thoroughly 3 times during cooking. At the end of cooking the pudding will have a thin skin and most of the liquid will have been absorbed. Serve warm, straight from the dish.

Cook's Notes

TIME
Preparation about 25 minutes, cooking 40 minutes. Cooling 5 minutes.

COOK'S TIP
Choose a fairly deep, wide dish.

SERVING IDEAS
Serve on its own or accompanied with stewed fruit. Or top each portion with a thick fruit preserve.

● 465 calories/1945 kj per portion

Eastern milk puddings

SERVES 6

1 tablespoon cornflour
2 tablespoons ground rice
600 ml/1 pint milk
50 g/2 oz sugar
2-3 teaspoons rosewater
50 g/2 oz ground almonds
15 g/½ oz chopped pistachio nuts,
to decorate

1 Put the cornflour and rice in a bowl and mix with a little milk.

2 Pour the remaining milk into a saucepan, add the sugar and heat until the sugar has dissolved and the milk is almost at boiling point. Pour the milk on to the paste, stirring constantly, then return to the pan and bring slowly to simmering point, stirring all the time.

3 Simmer gently for about 3 minutes, stirring constantly until the mixture begins to thicken slightly and coats the back of the spoon.

4 Add the rosewater and cook, stirring, for 2 minutes, then whisk in the almonds with a balloon whisk until smooth. Remove from heat.

5 Pour the custard into 6 individual dishes. Allow to cool, then cover and refrigerate for 2 hours until firm. Decorate with the chopped pistachio nuts just before serving.

Cook's Notes

TIME
20 minutes preparation, plus 2 hours chilling.

VARIATION
If pistachios are not available, use walnuts instead.

● 150 calories/625 kj per portion

Rhubarb rice mould

SERVES 4-6
540 g/1 lb 3 oz can rhubarb, drained with 150 ml/¼ pint syrup reserved (see Cook's tip)
450 g/15½ oz can creamed rice
few drops of vanilla flavouring
1 rounded tablespoon (1 sachet) powdered gelatine

1 Rinse out a 1 L/1¾ pint mould with cold water, shake off the excess moisture, then refrigerate.
2 Place the drained rhubarb, rice and vanilla in a large bowl and mix gently together.
3 Sprinkle the gelatine over the reserved rhubarb syrup in a heatproof bowl. Leave to soak for 5 minutes until spongy, then stand the bowl in a pan of gently simmering water for 1-2 minutes, stirring occasionally, until the gelatine has dissolved.
4 Cool the gelatine slightly, then pour it in a thin stream on to the rhubarb mixture, stirring constantly with a large metal spoon. Spoon the mixture into the prepared mould, cover with cling film and refrigerate for 3-4 hours, until set.
5 To unmould the dessert: loosen the edges of the mixture from the sides of the mould with your fingers. Dip the mould into a bowl of hot water for 1-2 seconds, then invert a dampened plate on top. Hold the mould and plate firmly and invert, giving a sharp shake halfway round. Lift off the mould.
6 Allow the dessert to stand at room temperature for about 30 minutes before serving.

Cook's Notes

 TIME
15 minutes preparation, plus 3-4 hours setting time and 30 minutes standing at room temperature.

 COOK'S TIP
Using canned rhubarb makes this an easy-to-prepare dessert. If you want to make it with fresh rhubarb, place 350 g/12 oz trimmed, chopped stalks in an enamel or other lined saucepan. Add 150 ml/¼ pint water and sugar to taste, then cover and cook gently until the rhubarb is tender. Cool completely, then drain well, reserving 150 ml/¼ pint of the cooking liquid.

●190 calories/800 kj per portion

Flaky rice sundae

SERVES 4
600 ml/1 pint milk
50 g/2 oz flaked rice (see Buying guide)
25 g/1 oz sugar
few drops of vanilla flavouring

TOPPING
15 g/½ oz margarine or butter
1 tablespoon golden syrup
25 g/1 oz corn flakes or rice crispies

1 Pour the milk into a medium heavy-based saucepan. Bring slowly to simmering point over low heat, then sprinkle in the flaked rice. Simmer gently, stirring frequently, for 15-20 minutes, until the rice is tender and thickened. ⚠

2 Remove from the heat and stir in the sugar and vanilla, to taste. Cool slightly, then spoon into 4 dessert dishes. Leave to cool completely.

3 Make the topping: melt the margarine with the syrup in a saucepan over low heat. Remove from the heat, add the corn flakes and stir gently with a large metal spoon until evenly coated.

4 Spoon the topping over the puddings. ⚠ Leave to set about 30 minutes before serving.

Cook's Notes

 TIME
35 minutes preparation, plus cooling time.

 BUYING GUIDE
You can buy white and brown rice flakes. The brown variety, which are sold in health food stores, have a pleasant 'nutty' flavour and more food value.

 WATCHPOINTS
The milk should only simmer gently, otherwise it will evaporate and the pudding will be too thick.

The topping sticks together and hardens as it cools, so it must be divided between the dishes while still warm.

 SERVING IDEAS
This easy-to-make milk pudding with its tempting crisp, sweet topping can also be served hot. Spoon the pudding into the dishes, but do not cool; make and add the topping, then serve at once.

 VARIATIONS
Try this topping over other milk puddings (canned, if liked), such as sago or semolina.

● 240 calories/1000 kj per portion

Peach rice condé

SERVES 6
75 g/ 3 oz pudding rice, rinsed and
   well drained
4 tablespoons sugar
1 L/2 pints milk
300 ml/½ pint double cream
½ teaspoon vanilla flavouring
4 tablespoons raspberry jam
825 g/1 lb 13 oz can peach halves,
   well drained

1 Put the rice, sugar and milk into a large saucepan. Partially cover the pan and cook over very low heat for about 1 hour, stirring regularly, until the rice is soft and has absorbed almost all of the milk. [!]
2 Pour the cooked rice into a large bowl. Cover the surface closely with cling film to prevent a skin forming, then set the rice aside to cool completely (see Cook's tip).
3 Whip the cream until it forms soft peaks. Fold half of the cream and the vanilla flavouring into the cold rice, then spoon into a serving dish and level the surface.
4 Sieve the raspberry jam into a small saucepan and heat gently until melted. Remove from the heat.
5 Arrange the peach halves, cut side down, on top of the rice, leaving a small border around the edge. Brush the peaches with the warmed jam.
6 Pipe or spoon the remaining cream neatly around the edge of the rice and in the centre. Serve cold.

Cook's Notes

TIME
30 minutes preparation, about 1 hour cooking, plus several hours cooling, preferably overnight.

VARIATIONS
Canned pears, apricots or pineapple can be used instead of peaches.

COOK'S TIP
Prepare the rice up to the end of stage 2 the day before you intend serving the pudding. Keep it in the refrigerator until ready to finish.

[!] **WATCHPOINT**
The rice must be stirred frequently during the cooking to prevent it sticking. The cooked rice should be creamy and thick enough to support the weight of the peaches, if it is too runny, drain off all the surplus liquid before cooling.

●485 calories/2025 kj per portion

Creamy Danish rice

SERVES 4-6

90 g/3½ oz pudding rice
425 ml/¾ pint high-cream milk (see Buying guide)
20 g/¾ oz caster sugar
150 ml/¼ pint whipping cream
50 g/2 oz blanched almonds, very finely chopped
1 teaspoon vanilla flavouring
1 tablespoon sweet sherry (optional)

1 Bring the milk slowly to the boil in a heavy-based saucepan. Add the rice and sugar and stir well. Cover the pan and cook as gently as possible for about 45 minutes, stirring frequently, until the rice is cooked and tender. [!]

2 Turn the cooked rice into a wide bowl and leave until completely cold, stirring occasionally to prevent a skin forming on top.

3 Whip the cream until it just forms soft peaks. Using a large metal spoon, fold the cream into the rice, then fold in the almonds, reserving 1 tablespoon for decoration. Fold in the vanilla and sherry, if using.

4 Spoon the mixture into a serving dish, cover and refrigerate for at least 30 minutes. Serve the pudding chilled, sprinkled with the reserved almonds (see Serving ideas).

Cook's Notes

TIME
Preparation takes about 40 minutes, but allow about 2 hours for the rice to cool and at least 30 minutes chilling time for the pudding.

WATCHPOINT
Keep an eye on the rice, especially towards the end of cooking time, and stir regularly to prevent it sticking. When cooked, the rice should be soft, but not mushy.

DID YOU KNOW
In Denmark this rice pudding is traditionally served on Christmas Eve. A whole blanched almond may be buried in the pudding just before it is served: the person who finds it is given a present and the belief is that if a young girl finds it she will soon marry.

SERVING IDEAS
Serve the pudding with poached fruit, or with a tart fresh fruit to offset its creamy richness.

BUYING GUIDE
High-cream milk is sold in bottles with a gold or striped green and gold top. It is also available in cartons. Ordinary pasteurized milk can be used instead, but will give a slightly less rich result.

● 375 calories/1575 kj per portion

Quick peach crisp

SERVES 4

820 g/1 lb 13 oz can peach slices,
drained, syrup reserved
25 g/1 oz rice crispies, lightly
crushed (see Cook's tips)
75 g/3 oz light soft brown sugar
65 g/2½ oz margarine or butter,
melted
25 g/1 oz plain flour
¾ teaspoon ground mixed spice
pinch of salt

1 Heat the oven to 180C/350F/Gas 4.
2 Put the peaches and 2 tablespoons
reserved syrup into a 1 L/2 pint
ovenproof dish.
3 Mix together the remaining ingredients and sprinkle over the peaches.
Press down lightly all over.
4 Bake in the oven for 30 minutes
until golden. Serve hot.

Cook's Notes

TIME
Preparation 15 minutes,
cooking time about 30
minutes.

COOK'S TIPS
Crush the rice crispies
by squeezing handfuls
of them in your fist.
This dessert is a useful standby that can be quickly made from
store-cupboard ingredients.

VARIATIONS
Use other canned fruit,
such as apricots or
pears.

SERVING IDEAS
Serve with soured
cream, natural yoghurt
or vanilla ice cream.

ECONOMY
Save the extra syrup and
use it for a fruit salad or,
frozen in special containers, it
makes unusual ice lollipops for
children.

●295 calories/1225 kj per portion

Crispie gâteau

MAKES 6-8 SLICES
150 g/5 oz rice crispies
75 g/3 oz margarine
75 g/3 oz marshmallows
75 g/3 oz plain toffees
vegetable oil, for greasing

FILLING
½ tablespoon powdered gelatine
3 tablespoons water
600 ml/1 pint cold milk (see
   Watchpoints)
2 × 67 g/2½ oz packets butterscotch
   dessert mix
2 small bananas
1 teaspoon lemon juice
215 g/7½ oz can peach slices,
   drained

1 Lightly oil a 20 cm/8 inch springform cake tin. Put the rice crispies into a large bowl.

2 Put the margarine, marshmallows and toffees into a heavy-based pan. Heat gently, stirring occasionally, until melted, then beat until smooth. Pour on to the rice crispies and mix until evenly blended.

3 With the back of a large metal spoon press the crispie mixture evenly over the base and sides of the prepared tin. Leave in a cool place for at least 2 hours to firm.

4 Make the filling: sprinkle the gelatine over the water in a small heatproof bowl. Leave to soak for 5 minutes, then stand bowl in a pan of gently simmering water for 1-2 minutes, stirring occasionally, until gelatine has dissolved. Remove bowl from pan.

5 Pour the milk into a large bowl and whisk in butterscotch mixes. Leave for 1 minute until thickened, then fold in gelatine.

6 Slice the bananas, then cut each slice across into 3 strips. Toss in lemon juice, then fold into butterscotch mixture. Refrigerate for 1 hour, or until on point of setting.

7 Carefully remove crispie case from tin and place on a serving plate. Turn butterscotch mixture into case and level the surface. Leave in a cool place for about 1 hour, until set. Arrange the peach slices over the filling and serve at once.

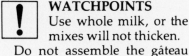

Cook's Notes

TIME
45 minutes preparation, plus 2 hours for the case to firm and a further 2 hours for the filling to set.

WATCHPOINTS
Use whole milk, or the mixes will not thicken.
Do not assemble the gâteau more than 1 hour before serving or the crispie case will soften.

 SERVING IDEAS
This pudding-cum-cake is ideal for a tea-party; tie a ribbon around the sides for a more festive look.

● 490 calories/2050 kj per slice

Chocolate nutty tapioca

SERVES 4

40 g/1½ oz flaked tapioca (see Did
  you know)
600 ml/1 pint milk
25 g/1 oz light soft brown sugar

TOPPING

25 g/1 oz raw peanuts, skinned and
  coarsely chopped
25 g/1 oz plain chocolate, coarsely
  grated

1 Put the tapioca into a medium
heavy-based pan and pour in plenty
of cold water. Bring to the boil,
simmer for 5 minutes, then drain
and return to pan (see Cook's tip).
2 Pour in the milk and bring slowly
to simmering point. Cook, stirring

frequently, for 45-60 minutes, until
the tapioca is clear and the mixture
is thick and creamy. Remove from
the heat and stir in the sugar, to
taste.
3 Heat the grill to moderate.
4 Turn the tapioca mixture into a

shallow, flameproof dish. Level the
surface, then sprinkle with the
chopped peanuts and grated
chocolate. Grill for 1-2 minutes,
until the chocolate is melted and the
nuts are lightly browned.
5 Serve the pudding hot or cold.

Cook's Notes

TIME
This easy-to-make pud-
ding takes just over
1 hour to prepare and cook.

DID YOU KNOW
Tapioca comes from the
root of the cassava plant,
widely grown in the West
Indies. It is sold in the form of
medium or tiny pearls as well as
flakes. Because of its high starch
content it will absorb more

liquid than some other grains,
and is sometimes also used in
savoury dishes such as soups or
stews to thicken them.

COOK'S TIP
The tapioca is cooked
briefly in boiling water
to soften it—otherwise the milk
might evaporate before it has
been absorbed.

● 235 calories/975 kj per portion

Blackcurrant semolina

SERVES 4
600 ml/1 pint milk
5 cm/2 inch stick cinnamon
50 g/2 oz caster sugar
75 g/3 oz semolina
2 egg yolks

TO FINISH
425 g/15 oz can blackcurrants
2 tablespoons double cream

1 Pour 425 ml/¾ pint of the milk into a heavy-based saucepan. Add the cinnamon stick, then stir in the sugar. Bring almost to the boil, then remove from the heat, cover and leave for 20 minutes to allow the milk to absorb the flavour of the cinnamon stick.

2 Put the semolina into a large bowl and slowly stir in the remaining milk, mixing well. Using a wire balloon whisk, beat in the egg yolks. Discard the cinnamon from the flavoured milk, then gradually stir the milk into the semolina mixture.

3 Pour the mixture into a clean, heavy-based saucepan and stir over very low heat for 5-7 minutes, or until thickened. ⚠ Immediately the first bubble appears, remove the pan from the heat and continue stirring for a further 2 minutes until the mixture is slightly cooled.

4 Pour the semolina mixture into an 850 ml/1½ pint glass serving bowl. Cover closely with cling film and refrigerate for at least 3 hours, or overnight, to firm.

5 Purée the blackcurrants and their syrup in a blender, then work purée through a nylon sieve to remove any tough bits of skin. Refrigerate the pureé until ready to serve.

6 To serve: uncover the semolina, spread the blackcurrant purée evenly over the surface, then lightly swirl the cream on the top.

Cook's Notes

TIME
35 minutes preparation (including standing time for the milk), plus at least 3 hours chilling. Allow about 5 minutes to finish.

! WATCHPOINT
Stir the semolina mixture constantly and do not allow it to come to the boil, or the egg yolks will scramble.

VARIATIONS
Instead of using a large bowl, divide the semolina mixture between 4 ramekins, or individual glass serving dishes.
Any thick fruit purée can be used instead of blackcurrant. A slightly tart purée is best.

●380 calories/1600 kj per portion

INDEX